PRAISE FOR

HUG OF WAR

"A groundbreaking guide for family business, *Hug of War* masterfully addresses the polarities which confront families in business. Cathy's pro tips alone are worth many times your investment. *Hug of War* is a gift to family enterprises and essential for advisors seeking to crack the code to unlocking planning paralysis and managing difficult family dynamics."

—**John A. Warnick**, Esq., founder, Purposeful Planning Institute

"Cathy Carroll, in *Hug of War*, asks us to embrace polarity thinking and practice as skills families and their advisors can use to find great answers to resolving issues presented by competing business mindsets and family mindsets in family businesses. She succeeds wonderfully. I highly recommend her book."

—**James E. Hughes, Jr.**, author of *Family Wealth: Keeping it in the Family, Family: the Compact Among Generations*, and co-author of *Complete Family Wealth, Version Two*

"Being there in a front-row seat and sometimes the head of the table generates wisdom and compassion that can deliver tough love with a hug. This author embodies these traits generously and deftly. Realize that America's multigenerational family-owned businesses in total contribute $7.7 trillion annually to the US gross domestic product, accounting for 83.3 million jobs, or 59 percent of the country's private workforce (FEUSA 2023 Report). This book will endure for many years, pages tagged and highlighted to come back to when emotionally highjacked, for guidance and remembrance that two disparate things do coexist and it's our humanity that [sees] both flourish."

—**Janet M. Harvey**, CEO, inviteCHANGE, author of *From Tension to Transformation: A Leader's Guide to Generative Change*

"Cathy Carroll gets into some of the deepest and most important issues that confront members of a business family. Fortunately for every reader, she also provides useful and actionable advice. It's going to make a positive difference in the lives of many families."

—**Mitzi Perdue**, author of *How to Make Your Family Business Last across the Generations*

"Using captivating storytelling and actionable guidance, Carroll explores the many tangled relationships inherent in the family business landscape. Ultimately, she gives the reader reason to exhale, calmed in knowing that there is a way through the complexity. Applying the power of polarity thinking and both/and solutions, Cathy shares how families can find a path to supporting both business goals and family relationships. This book should be an arm's length away for every family business advisor and business-owning family member."

—**Kristin Keffeler**, chief learning officer, author of *The Myth of the Silver Spoon: Navigating Family Wealth & Creating an Impactful Life*, and co-author of *Wealth 3.0: The Future of Family Wealth Advising*

"Cathy Carroll's *Hug of War* provides a vital map for those navigating the complexities of working together while being family. With many relatable illustrations, readers will not only see themselves in this book but will also learn actionable ways to make forward progress."

—**Kristen Heaney**, MSW, BCC, family legacy coach, author of *In Three Generations: A Story about Family, Wealth, and Beating the Odds*

"Families in business often get stuck in a tug-of-war, with members battling for one option over another. Through vivid real-life examples, Carroll demonstrates how a 'both-and' perspective can often illuminate opportunities not previously recognized, help decrease conflict, and increase the enjoyment of doing business with family."

—**Melissa Mitchell-Blitch**, family business and family wealth consultant, author of *In the Company of Family: How to Thrive When Business IS Personal*

"*Hug of War* provides a unique and insightful perspective on the complexities of family businesses and the dynamics that arise from the interplay of family and business mindsets. As a family governance practitioner, I found the concepts of domain crossover, shadow influencers, and unorthodox power to be especially enlightening. The book's approach of framing challenges as polarities and offering practical strategies for managing them is a valuable resource for anyone working in the field of family governance. I highly recommend Hug of War to family business leaders and practitioners looking to navigate the delicate balance between family relationships and business success."

—**Tsitsi Mutendi**, co-founder, African Family Firms, author of *Raising the Baobab: A Collection of Tools for Multigenerational Wealth Building in Family Businesses*

"In *Hug of War*, Cathy Carroll masterfully simplifies the intertwined complexities of power, love, family, and business—without being simplistic. This essential resource is invaluable for family business leaders or those who support them (i.e., consultants/coaches) to foster harmonious and sustainable growth."

—**Cliff Kayser**, chief learning officer, Polarity Partnerships

"*Hug of War: How to Lead a Family Business with Both Love and Logic* is a must-read for anyone who owns and operates a family-owned business, is a family member working within the business, and even the non-family employee of family-owned businesses. Cathy Carroll has offered a practical approach to recognizing, mapping, and leveraging the polarities that are present in every family-owned business. Cathy accurately describes and brings to life the tensions families experience and navigate on a day-to-day basis and provides an invaluable resource for navigating and managing them. If readers make the time to explore the polarities identified within the book as they appear within their specific context and apply the four-step process Cathy has laid out, they will be on the path to cultivating a stronger family and stronger business."

—**Dr. Tracy Christopherson**, co-founder, MissingLogic, LLC, co-author of Polarity Intelligence: The Missing Logic in Leadership

"Cathy Carroll's *Hug of War* is a book about family businesses, yes. But it's also a modern and fresh take on business in general, regardless of the corporate structure.

"Profound and illuminating, I found myself cringing at many of the examples Carroll weaves throughout the narrative. Of course, the cringing came from the all-too-familiar elements of each example. She described a concept called 'elder power' and that hit me like a ton of bricks!

"Perhaps most significantly, *Hug of War* offers a series of helpful tips and techniques to shape today's leaders and their skillset. Roughly fifteen years ago, I decided to tear our family business in two; Hug of War would have been the go-to resource I needed to ensure the best possible outcome."

—**Brian Burkhart**, founder and CEO, SquarePlanet, author of *Stand for Something: The Power of Building a Brand People Authentically Love*

"*Hug of War* is drawn from Cathy's experience leading a successful family business, and it's written from the front lines of family businesses where she is hired to ask the tough questions that will help family members find a path forward. The issues Cathy examines, the questions she poses, and the tips she provides add up to a practical playbook that can inform and guide any family business leader on their own journey of complexity and emotion."

—**Greg Bustin**, business consultant, executive coach, author of *Accountability: The Key to Driving a High-Performance Culture*

"I wholeheartedly recommend *Hug of War* by Cathy Carroll as a personal and practical guide for navigating the complexities of family businesses. At its core, this book delves into the intricacies of family dynamics, shedding light on the challenges and nuances that come with running a business within a familial context. Cathy Carroll effectively showcases the conflicting commitments that arise between the family mindset and business mindset polarity, offering valuable insights for those grappling with similar issues.

"What sets *Hug of War* apart is the author's raw vulnerability in sharing her personal story, making the narrative relatable and authentically engaging. The book provides a comprehensive guide for embracing and navigating these polarities, offering a four-step process that transcends tensions inherent in family businesses. Personally, Hug of War struck a chord with me, offering profound insights and practical strategies that have helped me navigate and understand my own family business dynamics better.

"If you're seeking a resource that combines personal anecdotes with actionable advice on successfully managing the intricate dance of family dynamics in business settings, *Hug of War* is a must-read. Cathy Carroll's expertise and heartfelt storytelling make this book a valuable companion for anyone looking to build stronger relationships and navigate the complexities of family businesses with grace and insight."

—**Daphne Jefferson**, principal and executive coach, Jefferson Consulting Group LLC, author of *Dropping the Mask: Connecting Leadership to Identity*

"In this book, Cathy immediately gets to the heart of the gifts and challenges of operating family businesses around the globe. Her references of the family mindset and business mindset help to illustrate the complexities that emerge, no matter the business. Cathy artfully illustrates and explores the polarities that exist with every family business and provides the reader with substantive examples and exercises to work through the 'tough stuff' of being in a family business. Every member of a family business should read this practical book. Readers will immediately take away sound ideas on how to navigate through the complexities that families face, in business."

—**Joan R. Hibdon**, executive coach, leadership consultant, author of *The Leader's Guide to Mastering Feedback: Transform Relationships and Results One Conversation at a Time*

"I'm pleased to see Cathy Carroll extend many of the concepts from Navigating Polarities into the domain that matters most to her: family business."

—**Kelly Lewis**, principal and founder, Lewis Leadership Group; board member, InnerWill Leadership Institute; co-author of *Navigating Polarities: Using Both/And Thinking to Lead Transformation*

"In *Hug of War*, Cathy highlights the countless polarities that arise as much in family offices as in family businesses. Her guidance on harmonizing polarities facilitates vertical development and supports growth in the triad of family office leadership: mindset, capacity and agility."

>—**Greg McCann**, founder and advisor, Generation6, lead editor and co-author of *Reshaping Reality: Unlocking the Potential of the Single Family Office*

"Cathy Carroll has written a cogent, accessible book that helps cut through the clutter and nonsense that often plagues books about family business. Perhaps because she has lived it herself, she understands firsthand what it is like to lead a family business in delicate transitions. Cathy has also done the hard work of reflecting on that experience and clearly and directly explains what makes being in business difficult and more importantly how to work to effectively manage the paradoxes and polarities that every family must address if they are going to both thrive in business and flourish as a family."

>—**Matt Wesley**, principal, The Lovins Group

Hug of War: How to Lead a Family Business with both Love and Logic
by Cathy Carroll

© Copyright 2024 Cathy Carroll

979-8-88824-364-0

All rights reserved. No part of this publication may be reproduced, stored in a retrieval system, or transmitted in any form or by any means—electronic, mechanical, photocopy, recording, or any other—except for brief quotations in printed reviews, without the prior written permission of the author.

Published by

◀ köehlerbooks™

3705 Shore Drive
Virginia Beach, VA 23455
800-435-4811
www.koehlerbooks.com

HUG of WAR

HOW to LEAD a FAMILY BUSINESS with *both* LOVE *and* LOGIC

CATHY CARROLL

VIRGINIA BEACH
CAPE CHARLES

Hug of War is dedicated to Wallace E. Carroll, his ancestors, his descendants, and all whose lives he touched.

TABLE OF CONTENTS

FOREWORD..x
INTRODUCTION..II

CHAPTER 1
Compensating Family...1

CHAPTER 2
Domain Crossover...17

CHAPTER 3
Shadow Influencers...35

CHAPTER 4
Unorthodox Power...53

CHAPTER 5
Integrating Privileges and Responsibilities...................65

CHAPTER 6
Fostering Constructive Conflict...................................79

CHAPTER 7
Resolving Common Dilemmas
in Leadership Succession..109

CHAPTER 8

Resolving Common Dilemmas
in Family Business Governance..129

CHAPTER 9

Embracing Polarities
to Harmonize Opposites..141

CHAPTER 10

Applying Polarity Principles
to Family Business...169

CHAPTER 11

Conclusion,
A Step Back and A Look Ahead..183

APPENDIX 1

Governance...187

APPENDIX 2

Family Business Polarity Assessment...197

FOREWORD
BY AMY SCHUMAN

Just picture it: On every continent. In every time zone. In every settlement, village, and city across the globe. In every language and climate. Families dream of making a business together, working side by side, supporting each other and their parents and children and even their children's children's children. Brothers and sisters and mothers and fathers, aunts and uncles and spouses and cousins, and best friends and next-door neighbors dream up new ways to do things together. They dedicate their blood, sweat, and tears to bringing these dreams to life.

With persistence, talent, and serendipity, many of these dreams come true. Not just the owning families but entire communities are strengthened as jobs are created and risks bring rewards well beyond the wildest imagination of the founders.

Wherever they live on the globe, families in business together face predictable challenges. Hard decisions must be made. Failures and missteps can threaten success and bring forward motion to a complete stop. Along with prosperity and innovation come tales of splintering families and cut-off relationships, ignored cousins, and injured in-laws.

I grew up in a family business where my father worked for his father-in-law, my grandpa, in a small electrical contracting business in Chicago. Having a business brought us together in many ways, and I remember the treat of going with my dad to his office on Saturday mornings. At the time, I had no idea of the family's struggle to do what was best for the business and for family relationships. But it's clear to me now that many "both/and" approaches were created to allow family members to *both* work together **and** enjoy holiday dinners together for many decades.

Later in life, as a key executive in a fourth-generation family-owned and -operated auto parts manufacturer, I saw the power of both/and solutions proven many times over. The owning family emphasized both people and profits. The plant achieved award-winning customer service, product design, and financial performance and modeled a corporate culture that featured on-site daycare, summer day camp for employees' children, and exceptionally low employee turnover. This manufacturer achieved *both* high-level business results *and* strong relationships.

Together with my colleagues at The Family Business Consulting Group, over the last twenty-five years, I've had the opportunity to help family firms and family offices manage the opportunities and challenges that come from working with loved ones. In many situations, the dilemmas appeared to be insurmountable. Disagreements about family and business endured over multiple generations, lasting beyond multiple leadership teams and family configurations. Smart, hardworking, and caring families try everything they can to solve the stubborn problems they face. They keep hitting brick walls. It can feel like the solutions they apply make their problems worse instead of better. Nothing makes the problems go away.

Most of the time, these problems don't go away because they aren't problems. They are polarities or paradoxes that cannot be solved with either/or solutions but must be managed with both/and approaches. They are inevitable, unavoidable, and natural dynamics that exist in all systems but are particularly conspicuous and troublesome in family enterprises.

In the pages of *Hug of War*, Cathy Carroll shares her wide-ranging experience with tough, complicated, and interpersonal relationships in family firms. If you've spent time with family firms, no matter what your role (owner, manager, family member, advisor, board member, etc.), you will be struck by the accuracy and realism of the examples she shares and the depth of understanding reflected in their recounting.

Cathy skillfully shows how these stubborn situations reflect paradoxes that require both/and solutions and test the patience and skill of those involved. Instead of being defeated by these seemingly impossible situations, Cathy and her clients use their knowledge of how to manage family business paradoxes to create paths forward that can preserve both family relationships and business performance.

In our book, *Family Business as Paradox*, John Ward, Stacy Stutz, and I explored how paradoxes show up in family enterprises. Like Cathy, we were inspired by the work of Barry Johnson and Polarity Partnerships (www.polaritypartnerships.com). Over the years, other prominent family business advisors, like Ivan Lansburg and Ken Moores (and renowned business consultants like Jim Collins and Roger Martin), have written about the importance of both/and approaches to managing tricky issues in family enterprises.

Cathy shares wonderful cases from her coaching experience that illustrate the poignant, comic, and tragic ways human beings get tangled up in their own best intentions. She draws a clear line between seemingly impossible challenges and the path forward provided by a polarity mindset and an appreciation of both/and approaches.

What inspires me about these cases is how universal they are. They are tales of human beings entangled in frustrating, complicated, and apparently impossible dilemmas with many of the most important people in their lives. By the end of this book, you will have a good understanding of practical and effective ways to manage these paradoxes. And best of all, as I've found in my own family business experiences, the solutions they find often contain insights, innovations, and opportunities that would never have been seen without honoring the paradox. Happy reading!

"Yin and yang, male and female, strong and weak, rigid and tender, heaven and earth, light and darkness, thunder and lightning, cold and warmth, good and evil . . . the interplay of opposite principles constitutes the universe."

—Confucius

INTRODUCTION

While seated in the lobby of a new client's office, I heard a deep voice behind the closed door, booming with displeasure. Could this be my new client? *I wondered.* Soon after the bellowing ended, the office door opened, and Mike greeted me with slicked-back white hair and a kind yet exasperated smile. "Please come in," he said, gesturing toward the brown leather office couch. He sat in the armchair across from me.

"I just don't get it," Mike began. "This is my ninth startup, and I have never been more wrapped around the axle than I am right now." At fifty-nine years old, this highly successful, serial entrepreneur, husband, father, and grandfather was at his wit's end.

"I can't put my finger on it, but there is something different about working with family," Mike said. "I started this business to give my child a head start. We have so much potential, but I am ready to fire my entire staff."

Already, his voice was getting louder.

Mike didn't need this business. He had started and sold eight companies throughout his career, and his retirement was secure. He did it for his daughter, whom he loves dearly. She was bright but had a history of behavioral health challenges in her teens and twenties that had strained his marriage. Mike hoped that building and transferring this business to his daughter would secure her future.

Things were not going as planned. "They have this cavalier, arrogant attitude about work," he said, seeking my sympathy. "Here's an example. My son-in-law told me that I'm lucky to have him working here because he is the 'linchpin of this business.'"

Mike leaned forward, his eyes wide. "The linchpin? You've got to be kidding me. Most days, he shows up late, and when he is here, he berates the staff. Worst of all, he isn't even close to meeting his sales targets. Linchpin my ass." Mike groaned, leaning back and pushing his hand through his hair.

"It sounds like he's falling short of your expectations," I said. "You said earlier that you are ready to fire your entire staff. What's holding you back from firing him?"

Looking down, with a lowered voice, Mike replied, "I've been on the verge of firing him for months, but I won't do it. I can't. He's my daughter's husband and the father of my granddaughter. Both he and my daughter rely on this company for their income. If I fire him, he'll end up asking me for money anyway because he couldn't earn as much outside of this place as he earns here," Mike said. "Plus, my wife and I don't want them to move away with our granddaughter. If they left town, my wife would be devastated, and it would be my fault."

Mike felt boxed in, miserable, and exasperated. It was beginning to affect his health.

"This company has changed me," he said. "I haven't raised my voice in thirty years, and suddenly, I am losing my temper daily. What is happening to me?"

◆ ◆ ◆

Mike brought this challenge to our first coaching session. He was blindsided by the unique challenge of leadership in a family business—the competing commitments of family and business. When Mike wore his business hat, he knew what to do. *If these behaviors don't change, these people need to go.* And when Mike wore his family hat, he knew what to do. *I want to help my children flourish.* When he wore both hats at the same time, he felt befuddled, frustrated, and stuck, and he didn't understand why.

This true story is an example of one of the great dilemmas of family business[1]—reconciling the opposing forces of the family mindset and the business mindset. When using a family mindset, we think about fairness, belonging, and sharing. It's an emotional operating system that is driven by love. By contrast, when using a business mindset, we think about competition, profits, and meritocracy. It's a rational operating system that is driven by logic. Leaders in family businesses operate with both the family mindset and the business mindset *simultaneously*. These mindsets are fundamentally different and too often opposed, and family business leaders struggle to reconcile them.

These two operating systems in a family business form a polarity. Sometimes called a paradox, dilemma, dichotomy, duality, or conundrum, a polarity is a pair of opposite tendencies that need each other to exist. *Inhale :: Exhale* is a polarity, for example. So are *Ask :: Tell, Urgent :: Patient*, and *Candid :: Diplomatic*. Each pole of the polarity doesn't exist without the other. An inhale doesn't exist without an exhale.

In the case of a family business, the family and the business form a polarity[2] and drive opposing impulses. Family favors emotion; business favors reason. Acceptance into a family is unconditional;

---

1   I define a family business as any privately-owned business with at least one owner in the same family as another owner and/or employee.

2   Credit for using ':' to indicate a polarity goes to Kelly Lewis and Brian Emerson, authors of *Navigating Polarities: Using Both/And Thinking to Lead Transformation*, (Washington Paradoxical Press, 2019), 17. Further, family businesses are a chosen polarity, not a natural polarity.

acceptance into a business is contingent on performance. Family relationships are forever; business relationships are temporary. Siblings and cousins are generational equals; employees in a business operate in a hierarchy. It's like living in socialism and capitalism simultaneously.

Adding fuel to the fire, each member of a family business typically prefers one mindset over the other. Some family members favor the business over the family, whereas others favor the family over the business. As a result, different family members bring different *expectations* to decision-making, placing leaders into a cognitive fog and leaving the family in disharmony.

Leaders of public corporations have it easier. The fiduciary duty of the corporate officer is to maximize shareholder value.[3] Every decision has a backstop of which answer is most accretive to shareholders. The unique challenge of public company leadership is serving the masters of Wall Street every quarter.

In contrast, the blessing and curse of private enterprise is that profit is usually *one* of the goals, but often not the singular goal. Leaders of family businesses consider other priorities. Some priorities are easy to recognize: generous employee benefits, a healthy balance of work and life, and a commitment to the local community. Other priorities are less obvious, driven by unseen emotional needs such as playing by one's own rules or leaving a legacy. In the opening story, for example, Mike wanted the business to keep his family connected and his daughter financially secure. Regardless of the motivation, competing purposes, especially hidden ones, can create conflict within oneself and between people.

Successful leadership in a family business doesn't always follow the "best practices" found in leadership literature, which ignores this

---

3   The corporate world seems to be challenging the assumption that the sole purpose of business is profit maximization. In addition to profits, many capitalists are seeking a balanced set of values that are represented by the corporate social responsibility (CSR), environmental, social, and governance (ESG), B-Corporation, and the conscious capitalism movements, to name a few.

omnipresent family :: business polarity.[4] This book is intended to help family business leaders work through the challenges only they face, such as:

- How do you ensure your sister has the means to survive when the marketplace doesn't value her skills?
- How do you give a performance review to your mom when her skills have become obsolete and she's a drag on profits?
- How do you compensate siblings who bring different skills to the business but all come from the same family?
- How do you make reinvestment and dividend decisions when family owners have different values and/or stage-of-life needs?

These are the daily blocking-and-tackling challenges family business leaders face. This unique challenge became clear to me only after I left a twenty-year corporate career to join my family business.

My Family Business Leadership Adventure

My father and I met in the lobby of the hotel at 4:30 p.m. I brought some of his favorites: a plate of sharp cheddar cheese, expensive salami, and his favorite whiskey. I didn't want anyone's hunger to turn hangry.

"Dad, you've been talking about how you want to play more golf, spend more time fly-fishing, and travel with Tina," I said. [Tina is his second wife.] "I'd like to help you make that wish a reality. Let's, you and I, agree on performance metrics for the business, and then you hold me accountable to the results. Now that you are in your midseventies, I'd like to help you enjoy your life the way you want to while you also ensure the business thrives. What do you say?"

He stared at me with a confused look. "You mean I'm not involved?"

I replied, "I'd take the day-to-day burdens off your back while also

---

4   Throughout the book, I identify polarities by placing a double colon (::) between each pole of the polarity. There is no meaning to which word appears first. I could just as easily write "business :: family" as "family :: business."

keeping you well-informed. As much as you want to be. And I'd like to still come to you with questions and advice on occasion, but I'm asking for greater decision authority."

"Are you asking to be the CEO?" His voice grew loud, his words sharp.

"No. Not at all," I said. "My title is fine. It's just that after fifteen months following our strategic plan, you've started directing the team to follow a completely different strategy . . . one that we haven't discussed." His memory wasn't what it used to be, and it was starting to show. "It's confusing the team when we don't speak with one leadership voice. That's why I'm suggesting that I focus on the day-to-day, and you hold me accountable for results."

After a short pause, he turned to me, his cold, blue eyes staring directly into mine, and stated clearly, "Absolutely not. I am the CEO, and everybody needs to know it."

◆ ◆ ◆

I grew up in a family business. My grandfather was the original entrepreneur in our family, and although I grew up around his business, I spent my first twenty years after college as a pension actuary, an MBA student, and then a corporate executive in the travel industry. By 2009, I was a mid-level leader at United Airlines, and suddenly I got the call from my father inviting me to lead his businesses. (He owns five companies that sell sporting goods to team ropers—ropes and saddles, etc., for rodeo competitors.)

At the time, the companies were underperforming, and given my business background, he thought I could help. At first, I was ambivalent about the opportunity. I saw pros and cons from both the business mindset and the family mindset.

On the business side, the leading pro was that I was hungry for a new challenge and greater leadership responsibilities. The leading con was that my professional background was in the service industry, and these were manufacturing companies. That difference felt significant, and I'd face a steep learning curve if I joined. Plus, this *was* my first rodeo.

On the family side, the leading pro was that, by turning the businesses around, I would have a chance to be the family hero. That excited me. The leading con was working for my father. Our father-daughter relationship wasn't particularly warm, and I was reluctant to make myself financially and emotionally vulnerable to him.

After many conversations with both of my parents (who had divorced fifteen years earlier) and my four siblings (most of whom encouraged me to say yes), I accepted my father's offer and joined the company as president and COO. He receded into a strategic oversight role, and within a few years, the companies were thriving. We were nicely profitable. We had low attrition. Our efforts were paying off, and we were having fun along the way. Happiness ever after, right?

Six months later, my father suddenly reengaged with the business and ordered the general managers (who reported to me) to pursue significant changes in strategy with no explanation. The GMs and I were confused, especially since my father had participated in and approved the strategic plan. I'd made sure of it! After a handful of additional, illogical demands and several difficult conversations, I realized that the irrational behavior that I remembered from childhood was repeating itself in the family business today. Early memories of the loss of control and the inability to influence positive outcomes flooded back, leaving me sick to my stomach. So, I asked to meet with him in the lobby of the hotel at 4:30 p.m.

"Absolutely not. I am the CEO, and everybody needs to know it."

That wasn't the reply I'd hoped for. At that moment, I knew I'd lost the ability to lead. I'd had it for almost three years, but it was now gone. The conversation continued for a few more minutes, but in the end, I chose to resign. The conversation wasn't heated. It wasn't angry. It was calm and definitive.

But honestly, I was crushed. What just happened? What wasn't working for my father? The businesses were strong. My father's behavior wasn't logical. All I knew was that I had failed the business, I had failed the family, and I had to find a new career. This led to a long period of self-reflection, striving to make sense of what had happened. A few notions emerged.

The first relates to my father. Once I grew into this new leadership role, I unwittingly interfered with something more important to my father than profits. I wedged myself between my father and his friends because as the business grew stronger, the GMs communicated with me more than with him. That wouldn't have been a problem using the business mindset—they were in regular communication with their manager, me. But these GMs were more than business leaders to him. They were his closest friends. As he felt these friendships fading, he needed to reassert his relevance. Lose friendships to his daughter? No way. He lost friendships to his wife (my mom) when they divorced. No way he'd feel that pain again—he'd rather lose money than friends.

The second discovery relates to me, and this one took longer to recognize because it involved acknowledging my responsibility for what took place. I, too, was driven by ego. My vision of being the family hero was, in part, proving that I was "right."

You see, my father and I had different leadership instincts. He favored a more authoritative, unilateral leadership style that often manifests with a pounding fist and a raised voice—a classic command and control leadership style that was popular in the 1950s. Of course, his leadership style at work mirrored his parenting style at home, so it's no surprise that I grew to favor a more collaborative, transparent leadership style, focused on building strategic alignment and strong relationships.

In fact, I favored the opposite of almost everything my father represented. He preferred bold; I preferred humble. He loved spending; I loved saving. He cherished disruption; I strove for stability. So, when I finally joined the family business, I was on an unconscious quest to prove that *I was right* and that my leadership style could be successful. Not only did I want my father's friends, the GMs, to appreciate my leadership, but I also wanted them to value it *more* than they valued his. I wanted them to side with me. I wanted vindication.

I used the business domain as a proxy war for unresolved issues in the family domain.

Once I was able to see that truth within myself, I saw it repeat in countless ways with my family business coaching clients. I didn't realize that my father and I were struggling with polarities. We were on opposite sides of every dilemma. Had we recognized these tensions as simply polarities, we might have transcended our differences and integrated our opposing points of view to get the best of both. I have grown to appreciate the value of bold leadership, the need for strategic spending, and the benefits of disrupting the status quo. I couldn't see it before.

That is why I wrote this book. My hope is that other family business leaders grasp this concept faster than I did—and with far less suffering.

How to Read This Book

The title, *Hug of War,* is highly metaphorical and represents the core polarity with which family business leaders struggle. *Hug* represents the family mindset, driven by love. *War* represents the business mindset, driven by logic. Further, *Hug of War* also alludes to the tug-of-war tension leaders feel with both mindsets operating simultaneously in a family business.

Hug of War[5] is organized as follows. Chapter 1 explores a simple example of how the tension of the family mindset and the business mindset manifests in setting compensation for family members. Chapters 2, 3, and 4 describe how these different mindsets result in unusual power dynamics that I call domain crossover, shadow influencers and unorthodox power, respectively. Chapter 5 illustrates

---
5   This book is also filled with stories which are based on research with hundreds of families, some of whom I interviewed by phone just once, some I worked with for years, and some are drawn from public media. Most identities have been masked.

the internal anguish that the family mindset :: business mindset polarity presents, and chapter 6 illustrates how that same polarity leads to conflict within the family. While chapter 7 explores various polarities in family business succession, chapter 8 describes multiple polarities that arise in family business governance. Finally, chapter 9, "Embracing Polarities to Harmonize Opposites," culminates in a list of ten polarity principles to support your understanding of how they work, and chapter 10 provides a four-step process (with examples) to transcend the tensions inherent in family businesses. *I sincerely hope you read chapters 9 and 10 before shelving this book, even if you skip ahead to do so.* These chapters are very different from the others and contain the most applicable insights in the book. Finally, chapter 11 zooms out and looks ahead.

Although *Hug of War* is focused on leadership in family businesses, the strategies are equivalently relevant for enterprising families with family offices and any family actively engaged in estate planning. This book won't tell you the "one right way" to lead a family business—because, as with any polarity, there is no "one right way." Instead, it's designed to help leaders see a fuller picture, not just half the story, so true harmony is within reach. As Ken Wilber, American theorist and author of *A Theory of Everything*, wrote, "When the opposites are realized to be one, discord melts into concord, battles become dances, and old enemies become lovers."

Let's dance.

"The test of a first-rate intelligence is the ability to hold two opposed ideas in mind at the same time and still retain the ability to function."

—F. Scott Fitzgerald

CHAPTER 1
COMPENSATING FAMILY

"Where's Jerome?" asked Henry as he stared out the office window at the company name, his last name, on the red sign at the curb. "Once again, he missed the strategy meeting."

"I don't know. He said he'd be here," replied Henry's brother cautiously, sensing Henry's growing frustration with their cousin, Jerome.

"I've had it!" Henry growled. "Grandpa is surely turning in his grave. It would kill him to see his grandson saunter in and out of this office with such entitlement."

All too familiar, Henry's resentment tapes started to roll. As CEO, with all the responsibility, how is it fair that he and Jerome earn the same salary, when Jerome barely shows up to work?

"It's like I wear a three-sided pirate hat: son, owner, and employee, but Jerome only wears one hat: owner. Somehow, his hat gives him license to do whatever he wants. Jerome wants all the benefits and none of the responsibility," said Henry. "Remember when he assaulted Frank in the marketing summit last year? I should have fired him then."

"Well, why don't you?" his brother asked.

Henry explained, "You know I can't fire Jerome. That would hurt his kid." Jerome had a special needs child who required expensive care, and Jerome needed the income. "You know he can't earn the same salary outside our family business."

Henry had exhausted every avenue to help Jerome. He'd hired consultants and psychologists. He asked Jerome to take a month off. He even offered to step down as CEO and bring in a nonfamily CEO to lead. Nothing worked. He had only one last move.

"I quit," said Henry. "This isn't worth it." He walked out the door, got into his car, and drove away.

◆ ◆ ◆

The Paradox of Leadership in Family Businesses

I start with this story because it sets up many of the ways this family mindset :: business mindset paradox manifests in family businesses. Henry has two competing sets of rules in his head. One set of rules compels him to terminate his employee. The other compels him to provide for his cousin. He is so stuck; his only option is to leave.

Family Mindset
I must support my cousin, Jerome.

Business Mindset
I must fire my employee, Jerome.

I have found equal compensation for family employees to be surprisingly common. Although the business mindset assumes compensation is a meritocracy, the family mindset assumes fairness sets pay, and many family members believe fair means equal. Here's how it makes sense from the eyes of a parent:

Family Mindset

Of course, I should pay my children the same. Otherwise, they will think I don't love them the same.

Business Mindset

Of course, I should pay my employees a market wage. That's what businesses do.

It's a competition between two "rights." Logically, it is "right" to pay market wages based on the business mindset, and emotionally, it feels "right" to pay equal wages based on the family mindset. That's what makes polarities so hard to grasp—both opposing views are right, and it's hard for our brains to hold two opposing truths at the same time.

Dylan, a serial entrepreneur, describes the family mindset well. He brought all three sons into the business, at the insistence of his wife. Their youngest "has the vision. He wants to do this [work] with me." The other sons aren't that interested, but Dylan's wife insists that he not play favorites. "My wife is especially sensitive. She would count the M&Ms at Easter to make sure they were equal. We can't show we love one son more than the other. She has a problem with unequal behavior toward the kids, and my wife is a strong, forceful person," Dylan says.

Even the concept of who determines pay is tripped up by these opposing rules. For example, the business mindset says that a leader sets compensation for her employees. However, the family mindset says, "Hey there, sister, you don't get to determine what I'm worth just because you're the CEO."

When Paulo (age thirty-three, G2)[6] joined his father's business after eight years at a global accounting firm, he had been earning more than his sister, Sofia (age thirty-six), who had joined their father's business right out of college. So, when Paulo joined with lateral pay,

---

6   Throughout this book, I'll refer to family member generations in the form of G#. For example, the founding generation is G1, their children in the second generation are G2, the grandchildren are G3, etc.

Sofia insisted that her pay be increased to Paulo's level. Then, five years later, Sofia changed her tune. She argued that she should earn *more* than Paulo because she had more children to put through school than Paulo did. For Sofia, the family mindset was in the driver's seat. For Paulo? The business mindset led, and he was livid because an increase in her pay was a decrease in the company's contribution to their profit-sharing plan.

PRO TIP

Why all this fuzzy thinking when emotions arise? It is a brain phenomenon called an "amygdala hijack,"[7] and it works like this: When our senses perceive stimuli, they pass through the amygdala (part of the brain's limbic, emotional system) before arriving at the prefrontal cortex where conscious control and decision-making takes place. When the amygdala interprets a stimulus as dangerous, it triggers the fight-or-flight response. Our body releases the stress hormones cortisol and adrenaline, our heart rate increases, we grow short of breath, and our pupils dilate to aid in securing immediate safety.

This biological response to danger served humanity well in the fang-and-claw world of constant survival. Unfortunately, our biology hasn't quite kept up with modern HVAC systems, industrialized agriculture, and indoor plumbing. Our basic food, clothing, and shelter needs[8] are typically met in the twenty-first century. However, our brains still produce a fight/flight/freeze/fawn[9] response when we misinterpret an email, when we're caught in heavy traffic, or when our siblings push our hot buttons.

When our amygdala is hijacked, we lose access to complex

---

7   "Amygdala hijack," Wikipedia, accessed March 2, 2024, https://en.wikipedia.org/wiki/Amygdala_hijack.
8   In wealthy economies, at least.
9   "Fight, Flight, Freeze, Or Fawn: How We Respond To Threats," SimplyPsychology, accessed March 2, 2024, https://www.simplypsychology.org/fight-flight-freeze-fawn.html.

decision-making capacities. We feel disoriented, and we see only one point of view—our own. It's tempting to believe that our rational brains are in the lead, but our emotions are driving our behaviors. (Studies show that even when calm and centered, emotions play a central role in decision-making.[10] Research shows we make choices based on emotion and then find logic to justify them.[11])

Strong emotion leads to compulsive reactions, not reasoned responses. For example, we have all received that email. The one that really gets under our skin. Our first instinct is to bang out an angry reply. It feels so good to get it out. But what happens when we hit send? We exacerbate the problem.

Many of us have developed the ability to self-manage. After we craft our heated response, we "save as draft" and come back to it an hour, a day, or a week later. Or we don't send it at all. If we return with our executive functions restored, we rewrite the email and problem-solve constructively.

Although this phenomenon happens to everyone, not just leaders in family businesses, I believe family businesses provoke the deepest, most powerful amygdala hijacks due to the intersection of love and money. This is why family business leaders have the most to gain from enhancing their emotional intelligence.

BOTTOM LINE: WHEN YOU HAVE BEEN TRIGGERED AND YOUR AMYGDALA HAS BEEN HIJACKED, PAUSE AND LET THE STRESS HORMONES ABATE BEFORE YOU CHOOSE YOUR RESPONSE.

---

10 Antonio Damasio, "The quest to understand consciousness," *TED*, March 2011, accessed March 2, 2024, https://www.ted.com/talks/antonio_damasio_the_quest_to_understand_consciousness.
11 "Motivated Reasoning," Wikipedia, accessed March 2, 2024, https://en.wikipedia.org/wiki/Motivated_reasoning.

Socialism and Capitalism

Working in a family business can feel like living in socialism and capitalism at the same time. The family mindset resembles socialism, which values equality, sharing, and harmony. The business mindset resembles capitalism, which values competition, meritocracy, and profits. I'm often amused when a family business leader who self-describes as a devout, free-market capitalist insists on paying her children an equal wage. That is socialism in action!

Ashley, the CEO of her family's business, preferred to live a modest lifestyle and put profits back into the business. "That's how we were raised," she said. Convinced her sister, who works part-time, would spend any amount she received, Ashley hid the millions of dollars of company profits from her sister. Financial transparency "would force a confrontation that I want to avoid," Ashley stated. "My sister would demand a $300,000 salary for leading a few marketing projects. She doesn't understand risk and reward. She believes in socialism for family, not capitalism."

So, for the sake of family harmony, Ashley kept the financial performance of the company a secret. "If she saw our books, it would change the dynamics of our relationship forever," said Ashley. "It's more important that the family is together, with relationships preserved."

Ashley is managing a polarity, one that's quite common in family businesses—reveal :: conceal. She conceals information, rather than reveal it, for the sake of family harmony. Someday, she may experience the overuse of concealing if her sister ever learns the truth. Decades of hiding information could change their relationship forever. Ironically, her decision to conceal information may undermine trust, which can lead to the future she fears the most—a fractured family.

Switching From Equal Pay to Market-Based Pay

How should families pay themselves? It depends. Equal pay can be quite harmonious in a family, at least for a while. But when the fairness value arises, so does family tension because fairness is subjective.

Families who initially embrace equal pay eventually—usually by the third generation[12]—migrate to market-based pay. As a fifty-eight-year-old, G2 CEO Lucas earned the same salary as his siblings until his children, nieces, and nephews entered the scene. With nine of nineteen G3 family members working in the business, the business couldn't sustain equal wages for all family members, so they migrated to market-based pay. Nevertheless, "It's really hard on my dad. He wants everyone to have the same," says Lucas, who still carries some resentment for the days of equal pay. "For decades, I was paid the same as my siblings even though I'm leading the business. I've had all the responsibility without the commensurate pay."

Goldilocks Is Rare

Family business compensation policies are often a Papa Bear or Mama Bear affair. Rarely are they Goldilocks. Often, family members are consistently overpaid or consistently underpaid relative to market wages; it's rarely "just right." There are many family mindset and business mindset justifications for this.

Family mindset justifications (founded in emotion) include:
- *We underpay family members relative to the market because we don't want our children to be spoiled. This business isn't their personal bank.*
- *We overpay our family members because we can. It's one of the benefits of being a family business, so I pay them what they need to live a comfortable life. I don't want them to struggle if they don't have to.*

---

12 In his April 2018 white paper, *Resilience of 100-Year Family Enterprises*, Dennis T. Jaffe, PhD, describes a phenomenon whereby in the third generation, "family businesses" tend to become "enterprising families." He describes a "family business" as "one in which family needs and dynamics are primary" compared to an "enterprising family that stewards strong professional enterprises that run on clear, firm and effective business principles."

Business mindset justifications (founded in reason) include:
- *We pay below market because reinvesting profits in this business creates more long-term value.*
- *We pay above market to lower profits because reducing the value of the business makes intergenerational ownership transfer more tax efficient.*

I hear more complaints about underpayment than overpayment. As one family CEO shared, "We reinvest our profits into the business, so we don't have lots of cash and haven't given pay increases. Our wives hate it. They call themselves 'seaman widows' because they keep hearing, 'Don't worry, honey, our ship will come in.'"

This introduces another common family business tension—invest :: harvest. Reinvesting in a business can yield wonderful benefits in the long run. At the same time, leaders who overfocus on reinvestment and neglect dividends run the risk of generating resentment among family members who'd like to enjoy some of the harvest.

Although underpaying family members has some risks, so does overpaying. Overpaid family members who can't replicate their income outside of the family business can feel trapped. Loss of autonomy breeds anger, frustration, and resentment. Overpaying also makes it hard to let underperformers go, especially when leaders feel responsible for other family members. (Recall Henry's conundrum in the opening story of this chapter.) Last, high-performing family members tend to resent overpaid underperformers, especially when the overcompensation drags down the financial performance of the business.

The False Dichotomy of Family Business

Much time has been frittered arguing whether one's family business should be "family-first" or "business-first." In my opinion, this is the wrong question. In a family business, one doesn't exist without the other. Because they are interdependent, better questions are "How do we get both the upsides of family and the upsides of business? How do we ensure we aren't overfocused on one over the other?" (More about embracing polarities in chapter 9.)

A common mantra in family businesses is "Take care of the business, and it will take care of the family." Sure, healthy profits can hide many weaknesses in a system, but ignoring the needs of the family can be a risky strategy in the long run. The family side of the family business is an emotional system, and when strong emotions are in play, rational thought recedes into the background. Ignoring emotional family dynamics doesn't make them go away.

The opposite mantra is "Family is number one." Sure, prioritizing the needs of the family makes perfect sense—until the family's needs exceed the ability of the business to provide for them, and the business fails. If shutting down the business is acceptable to the entire family as a potential outcome of a "family-first" policy, then there is no problem. But rarely is that the case.

The family-first or business-first argument is a false dichotomy. As with any polarity, either pole taken to the extreme guarantees the downsides of its overuse. Although family businesses are a *chosen* polarity, the family and the business are interdependent pairs, and therefore, neither pole can be neglected. The task of family business leadership is learning how to manage the tension between the two. Chapters 9 and 10 show you how.

Values Can Be Polarities Too

Family-first or business-first conflict is an example of conflict born from opposing values, but it's not the only values-related conflict that surfaces in a family business. Coming from the same family doesn't always mean every member shares the same values. I certainly don't share all the values of my siblings.

Take my sister, for example. I'm a saver; she's a spender. For years, I judged her for living a "garishly opulent" lifestyle, and she judged me for being "absurdly stingy." Then one day, I realized that one value is no better than the other. She can afford her choices, so what business is it of mine to criticize her just because I wouldn't make the same choices?

Having different values in a family isn't an inherent problem until the family members with different values need to make decisions about shared assets. It's the *shared assets* that make family members interdependent, and this interdependence threatens individual autonomy. *That's when it gets emotional.*

Because families are interdependent systems, the behavior of one family member can affect the others. Like a mobile hanging from the ceiling, touch one part of the mobile, and the entire mobile moves. The more one family member moves the mobile, the more it impacts the rest of the family. Further, the more interdependent the family (the more the family relies on a single mobile), the greater the impact on others and, thus, the greater the likelihood of conflict.

Doing what's right for *you* as an individual may negatively impact what's right for the *family*, and conversely, meeting the needs of the *family* may negatively impact *you*. It's a me :: we polarity, and the vexing truth about polarities is that it's *both* "right" to meet your own needs *and* it's "right" to meet the needs of your family. Another family business paradox.

Andy, a twenty-eight-year-old G4 vice president, describes the burden of stewardship associated with family business leadership. "If I worked outside of the family business, I'd focus only on what's right for me," he said. "But as a leader in my family business, I have to focus on what's right for my family and our employees, at the expense of what's right for me."

There are countless values-based polarities that give rise to family business conflict:
- Investing profits for the future :: harvesting profits today
- Making a fortune :: making a living
- Rapid growth :: measured stability

- Daring :: cautious
- Tradition :: innovation
- Urgent :: patient
- Transparency :: privacy
- Structure :: flexibility
- Needs of leading generation :: needs of rising generation
- Seek debt to fuel growth :: reduce debt to reserve cash for other investments

The invest :: harvest tension with annual profits is quite common, especially given the different life stages of various family members. When a leader who values the long-term decides to invest a larger percentage of profits into the business to fuel future growth, today's shareholders are affected by reduced ownership dividends.

This tension also arises between generations. Whereas the senior generation often seeks to harvest profits to finance retirement, the rising generation wants to invest in new technologies or equipment to build long-term value.

Similarly, a leader who invests in operational efficiency and infrastructure will frustrate the family executive who values investment in sales and growth. A risk-seeking family business leader who pursues an aggressive marketing and sales strategy may unnerve the family member with a lower tolerance for risk.

Yannick, a G2 CEO, described it like this. "With great income comes great responsibility. Tied to this is getting alignment on what to do with the income the company generates. Reinvest in the company or take a dividend? My sister is paying college tuition now," he said. "There are generational challenges, stage-of-life issues. It's definitely tough."

The family mindset (*be good to family*) weighed on Yannick, who had the formal authority to allocate profits. He felt obligated to consider the financial needs and wants of his other family members. You can imagine then how tension grows when one family member has power over another. (More on that in chapter 2.)

These tensions quickly devolve into conflict because they are framed as a problem that has a right answer. Polarities don't have right answers. They are tensions to manage, and once the family reframes the issue from a problem to a polarity, the family can reengage using the polarity framework described in chapters 9 and 10 to establish a path forward.

Tensions to Manage

Returning to compensation, framing compensation as a polarity helps you to identify the upsides and overuses of equal pay as well as the upsides and overuses of unequal pay. Then you craft an innovative strategy that accrues the upsides of both equal and unequal pay. That might mean that everyone gets the same base salary, and individual family members are bonused based on performance. Alternatively, everyone earns market-based pay, paired with an annual dividend based on percentage ownership, not performance. There are many ways to construct a "both/and" solution.

Here's a story of how one family did it. Brothers Eli and Josh bought out their father's business in a 60 percent Eli and 40 percent Josh split, leading to years of anger and resentment before they found peace. "Compensation was a constant issue from the start," Josh said. "It comes down to what you think you are worth." Eli, nine years older than Josh, bought controlling interest and stepped into the CEO role, while Josh bought the remaining 40 percent and ran engineering. Both worked equally hard in the business, which grew to be very successful.

Each brother wanted to be fair but defined fair differently. Convinced ownership percentage was fair, Eli wanted to split profits sixty-forty. Convinced equal effort was fair, Josh wanted to split the profits fifty-fifty.

Every year, they'd quibble about the allocation of profits. At first, Eli gave Josh extra money to pacify Josh's feelings. "Everyone thinks they are worth more than they get," Eli laments. "But in a family business, it works better to treat people more equally. Everybody gets their little extra somewhere along the line. Someone has a high salary because of seniority or title; another gets more vacation if they value it more than money."

Eventually, Eli and Josh both grew to accept a sixty-forty split of profits, in line with their ownership percentage. "Eli treats me well," said Josh. "I wanted to buy ten percent from him, so we had a fifty-fifty split, but I don't care as much now. We talk like we are fifty-fifty, but every profit is split sixty-forty. He put in more money, he's older, and he's been here longer. At the end of the day, we take care of each other."

In harmonizing the family mindset and the business mindset, Eli and Josh found harmony in *both* their brotherhood *and* their co-ownership of the family business. What a great "both/and."

Henry and Jerome Update

Bzzzz. It was the fourth call in an hour, and Henry ignored it just like he did the first three. He continued sanding the bench he was building in his garage, enjoying the fall air.

"Henry, please answer your father's calls," pleaded Henry's wife, handing him a towel. "He and your uncle keep calling because they think you betrayed them by quitting. They are lost without you. Just call them back. Please."

"Betrayed them? They have some nerve," said Henry, agape. "If they weren't so conflict-avoidant . . . if they had dealt with Jerome when they should have . . . we wouldn't be in this mess. They expect me to do all the hard work in this family."

"It's true. They need you. What would it take for you to go back?" she asked.

With the demands of leadership no longer on Henry's shoulders, he'd had time to reflect on the last twenty years working in the business. Working in his garage was quite meditative for Henry. He had the space to think about the conditions under which he'd return to the business.

"The only way I'd go back is if we built a board. We need independent, nonfamily advisers who can help us with situations like this. I also want to hire someone who can teach our family how to manage conflict so I'm not the only one doing it."

Bzzzz. The phone rang for a fifth time. This time, Henry answered it.

Questions for Chapter 1

1. How do you compensate your family? Equal or market-based?
2. Which mindset do you tend to favor, the family mindset or the business mindset?
3. What are the overuses of your preferred mindset?
4. What are the benefits of the opposite mindset?
5. What mindset do other members of your family prefer?
6. What conflicts might you be experiencing based on opposing values?

"I've learned that power is not bad, but the abuse of power or using power over others is the opposite of courage; it's a desperate attempt to maintain a very fragile ego."

—*Atlas of the Heart*

by Brené Brown

CHAPTER 2
DOMAIN CROSSOVER

Hi, My name is Max. My father tells me I need an executive coach, but I promise you, he's *the one who needs a coach, not me. He demoted me at work because I didn't invite his new wife's children to my son's briss. That's just not fair!*

—*Max, age thirty-six, G2 Manager*

◆ ◆ ◆

Those are the first words I heard from Max, but not the last. At thirty-six, he had been working for his father for six months when his father suddenly demoted him due to a bitter feud with his new stepmother, Nancy. Fiercely ambitious and full of potential, Max couldn't believe his professional dreams were being thwarted due to family relationships.

When the family mindset and the business mindset compete in the same arena, power manifests in all sorts of surprising ways. The next three chapters explore three power dynamics.

- **Domain crossover**: when family members leverage one domain (business domain) to exact results in a different domain (family domain) or vice versa.
- **Shadow influencers**: when people who have no ownership or employment in a business nevertheless wield enormous power.
- **Unorthodox power**: when family hierarchy and business hierarchy become circular and decision authority becomes unclear.

We'll start with domain crossover.

Max's story is a simple and all too common example of the domain crossover dynamic in family businesses. Because family business members operate in two domains, the family and the business, they have two domains in which to wield "hard" power. Max's father made it clear that Max's professional advancement would come only once he developed a civil familial relationship with Nancy. Max's father exercised power in the business domain to influence Max's behavior in the family domain.

Domain crossover power can show up in surprising ways. Paula, a forty-two-year-old G3 CEO of her family business, enjoyed jogging to work and showering at the office. However, fearing for Paula's safety, her mother remodeled the office to remove the showers so Paula would be forced to drive instead. As Paula said, "Sometimes things from age twelve will show up when you're a forty-year-old CEO."

Compensation is commonly used as leverage. When Samantha, thirty-six, joined her father's business twelve years earlier, her father didn't like her spending habits, so he forced her to save. "When I got my first paycheck, it was way lower than I expected," Samantha complained. "My stepmother told me that they had decided I wasn't 'good with money,' so they put a portion of my compensation into a savings account. I couldn't believe it! I was twenty-four years old!"

That's the family mindset in action. A public corporation wouldn't have the power to divert a portion of an employee's salary into an inaccessible savings account without the employee's consent.

It's not just parents who try to control their children; children leverage power with their parents too. When Jakov, a seventy-two-year-old founder, ceded partial control of his business to his son, Ivan, Ivan wasn't satisfied. He wanted full control. To get his way, Ivan withheld access to Jakov's grandchildren until Jakov granted full control of the business to him.

Jakov was torn and terrified. "My wife is a wreck and pressuring me to concede, but I'm scared. Our retirement savings are held in these investments, and I can't give up control of my financial future. I'm not even confident my son is ready to take over this business," he said. Being on the receiving end of domain crossover can feel exceptionally vulnerable.

PRO TIP

Domain crossover power is hard power: overt, forceful, threatening, and coercive. Hard power (also called "power over") leverages fear to win and leaves others feeling power*less*. At its best, hard power is efficient and useful in an immediate crisis, such as moving someone away from danger. At its worst, hard power is abusive. It threatens our human need for agency and self-determination.

Although there is a place for hard power, the most effective leaders use it sparingly. Hard power makes us pull away from others because power *over* others undermines trust and followership, two essential elements of effective leadership. Plus, it suppresses innovation and is difficult to scale. Hard power can leave others feeling trapped, which doesn't bring out the best in humans, so use caution. You may meet your near-term needs, but you may not like your result in the long run.

Even when leaders have positional power due to their

title, research[13] shows that social intelligence and empathy are more helpful in acquiring and exercising power than force or manipulation. Hard power may have been needed, even expected, 500 years ago, but today's workforce doesn't respond well to carrot-and-stick leadership, *especially from family members*, because it violates the norms of the family mindset.

When you are tempted to use hard power, first determine if the circumstances justify its use. Is there a life-threatening emergency that necessitates the use of hard power? Next, determine if your use of hard power comes from a place of fear or love.[14] If it's from a place of fear, find other ways to manage your anxiety and explore soft power alternatives. If it's from a place of love, and it's an emergency, use it.

If you aren't sure whether the impulse to use hard power comes from fear or love, use this two-one-two[15] technique to gain clarity. The two-one-two technique is designed to calm your nervous system and clear out any metaphorical cobwebs before choosing your behavior. It works like this: settle into a comfortable position, and then close or lower your eyes.

- For two minutes, simply notice your breath.
- For one minute, imagine warm sunshine enveloping your heart with every inhale.
- For two minutes, focus attention on a person, place, or thing you deeply love.
- After the five-minute reflection, reconjure the situation at hand and ask yourself, "What would love do?"

When you are on the *receiving* end of hard power, first decide

---

13 "The Power Paradox," Greater Good Magazine, accessed March 2, 2024, https://greatergood.berkeley.edu/article/item/power_paradox.
14 Watch this three-minute video to assess whether you are acting out of fear (below the line) or love (above the line): https://conscious.is/video/locating-yourself-a-key-to-conscious-leadership
15 Credit: Alexander Caillet, founder of Correntus: https://corentus.com

if it's a problem. In the long run, it's always a problem, but in the short run, it can be helpful (e.g., emergencies). However, when hard power violates your personal boundaries, it's time for a brave conversation. (More on brave conversations in chapter 6.) Brené Brown describes boundaries simply as what is okay and what is not okay. If your boundaries are unclear or not yet spoken, establish them. Then hold them.

As Brené Brown writes, "I also learned that when you hold someone accountable for hurtful behaviors and they feel shame, that's not the same as shaming someone. I am responsible for holding you accountable in a respectful and productive way. I'm not responsible for your emotional reaction to that accountability."[16]

If your boundaries continue to be crossed, then, as with any quandary, you have four options[17]: deny, cope, change, or leave.

- Deny: you can pretend the quandary doesn't exist.
- Cope: you can tolerate the quandary.
- Change: you can change how you engage within the quandary.
- Leave: you can leave the quandary.

Choose the option that is most appropriate for your situation.

If the transgressions are severe and you struggle to leave the situation, seek the support of a therapist. As Brené Brown continues in *Atlas of the Heart*, ". . . subjecting ourselves to that behavior by choice doesn't make us tough—it's a sign of our own lack of self-worth." Love yourself enough to get the support you need.

BOTTOM LINE: BE CAUTIOUS ABOUT USING HARD POWER AND THOUGHTFUL IN HOW/IF YOU RESPOND TO HARD POWER.

---

16 Brené Brown, *Atlas of the Heart* (New York: Random House, 2021), xix
17 Credit: Tyler Burnett, LCSW - Four Options for Problem Solving

Beware the Consequences of Good Intentions

Masato's parents were worried. With the economy in a downturn when Masato graduated from school, they crafted what they thought was a brilliant plan: start a business so the family could work together and also provide Masato with a solid career. Masato didn't take to the idea, though. He had little interest in the industry. So, they made him an offer he couldn't refuse; join the business and earn one-third ownership.

Fast-forward twenty years, and the industry had changed dramatically. Technology had disrupted their business model, leaving his parents concerned about their retirement. Masato, now in his early forties, felt enormous pressure to save the business for his parents. The burden was so heavy that he grew hostile at work and home, fearing the business was failing, and if it did, his skills weren't transferable to other industries.

In living his parents' dream, he was living his own nightmare. He knew that this business would not see him and his family into the future, yet he lacked the confidence in his skills to strike out on his own.

He described "overwhelming disappointment that I let my parents down, disappointment at the impact on my marriage, disappointment that I'm not the dad I want to be to my children, and most of all, disappointment in myself for wasting my career." Using the business domain to address anxiety in the family domain didn't serve this family well at all.

You Can't Disentangle Family from Business in a Family Business

Because emotional needs from the family domain play out in the business, and emotional needs from the business domain play out in the family, one would think the simple solution is to separate these domains—keep family family; keep business business. Alas, reality is messier than that.

For example, when a family member resigns from a family business, the departure impacts the family as well as the business. It's not like quitting a corporate job. When you leave a corporate job, you find a different job and work with new people. Conversely, leaving a family business, especially when the departure is emotionally charged, impacts the family system.

Seamus joined his older brother's business right out of college, and "the next fourteen years felt like forty," he claims. "After fourteen years of getting yelled at, working fifteen-hour days, and never hearing a word of appreciation, I finally quit. I even gave him a six-week notice so that I could transfer my responsibilities to my replacement. Turns out, he had to hire four people to replace me," Seamus said.

That was eight years ago, and they haven't spoken since. "I couldn't be there any longer. It was destroying me. I had lost all my self-confidence. Leaving was the best thing I ever did for myself, but holidays with my parents are still really uncomfortable."

The stakes are high when you work in a family business. The decisions you make regarding work can affect the entire family for a lifetime. Sometimes generations.

Resigning From a Family Business Is Hard. Firing a Family Member Is Harder.

Resigning from a family business is one thing; firing a family member is another. Although firing *any* employee can be difficult for an experienced manager, firing a *family member* carries a much heavier weight due to the impact on the family domain.

When you fire your cousin from a job, you can't fire her from being your cousin. You remain family, which means you will likely see her at weddings, funerals, and holidays. Those gatherings can become highly charged, often for years. It's one reason family business leaders tolerate underperformance from family members. Sometimes, they can't bear to hurt the feelings of someone they love, sometimes, they want to avoid family disharmony, and sometimes, they are simply unwilling to be responsible for the setback of a family member. It violates the tacit family mindset rule: family looks out for family.

Conor, a fifty-one-year-old G2 COO, struggled to hold his brother accountable at work but felt powerless to let his brother go. His brother "acted as if he were immune from losing his job," which frustrated Conor to no end. But firing his brother would have financial ramifications for his parents. "My brother lives in a house that my father owns. If I fire my brother, how can he pay our father the rent he owes for the house?" Conor felt constrained in the business domain due to the impact on the family domain.

In another example, Thomas, a sixty-eight-year-old G4 CEO, struggled with his sister for decades. It was clear to everyone that Shirley's poor performance damaged the business, but his parents wouldn't think of letting her go. When Thomas became CEO, the situation worsened, so he hired a family business consultant to evaluate the situation. Thomas committed to resign if the consultant said that Thomas was the problem. Instead, the consultant determined that the business would be better served if Shirley were removed from direct client contact, so Thomas moved her into an internal role.

Unfortunately, problems persisted. "All the key people are frustrated with her," said Thomas. "She thinks she's holier than thou religiously, but she can be an absolute jerk, even cruel." Thomas won't terminate her due to the sense of family responsibility he carries. "If I fired her, she would probably take her life," he fears. "In my mind and heart, I'm running a professionally run family business, but the truth is, my business hat and family hat are in conflict."

Firing a Family Member Is Harder. Getting Fired by Family Is Hardest

Perhaps the only thing harder than firing a family member is *getting* fired by a family member. It is more than a blow to one's ego and income; it feels like rejection from the family, which violates the family norms of unconditional love and acceptance. It feels extremely personal.

Take Porter, a forty-six-year-old G2 VP who had worked at his father's business for five years. One day, the director of HR called him into the conference room. As Porter entered the room, he saw the CFO and the director of HR seated at the conference table, both looking uncomfortable. As Porter sat down, a voice from the conference room telephone broke the awkward silence. It was his father's attorney informing Porter that his job had been eliminated. Porter was fired by his father's outside attorney, not his own father/boss.

Porter was blindsided. Not only did he not see it coming, but getting fired in front of his colleagues by the family attorney was humiliating. Porter's father never called him or explained a thing. In the snap of a finger, Porter lost his job, his self-confidence, and the illusion of family cohesion. His father had been difficult growing up, but Porter never imagined it would come to this. To this day, seven years later, Porter is still reeling from the experience and hasn't regained his professional footing.

Craving Autonomy and Belonging at the Same Time

We humans suffer an innate paradox. We want to be free, to have agency, to control our destiny. Simultaneously, we want to be loved, to be accepted, to belong in our family. This autonomy :: belonging polarity underlies much of the friction of domain crossover, and the amount of the conflict seems inversely proportional to the trust in the family relationships. The lower the trust, the greater the discord.

Caroline learned that lesson the hard way. When she was named trustee of her grandfather's trust, her sister Belle became enraged. Belle didn't want Caroline to have control over Belle or Belle's children. It violated the sibling norm of equality from the family mindset. Fearing the loss of autonomy and privacy, Belle put her foot down. "Hell will freeze over before I let Caroline control me or my children's future. I want my assets separated immediately, and if I need to hire lawyers to do it, I will," Belle threatened.

Even though Caroline was well-qualified to be trustee and had good intentions for all, Belle didn't trust Caroline and wouldn't stand for the imbalance of power. Belle remained hostile toward Caroline until Caroline resigned as trustee. Without trust in their sibling relationship, the power imbalance chafed them both. Ironically, the more Belle insisted on autonomy, the more she threatened her sense of belonging because the rest of the family grew frustrated with her ire.

Financial leverage in the business domain is called an incentive. Financial leverage in the family domain feels like coercion, and those with siblings know how insufferable control by a sibling can feel.

Lost in Translation

With these dual business and family mindsets, what one family member says is not always what another one hears. Even simple things said with one mindset but heard with another can cause unnecessary heartache. Angela, a thirty-six-year-old entrepreneur, hired her financially savvy father to manage her books. As one would expect her bookkeeper to do, her father asked regular questions about her monthly financial performance, such as, "Why was there a revenue dip?" and "What drove the increase in labor expense this month?"

Her father couldn't understand why Angela grew defensive every time he asked a simple business question until he realized that he asked questions from the business mindset, and she heard questions through the family mindset. *Why is my father judging me? I made these decisions for good reasons*, she thought. Thankfully, Angela could see the absurdity of her self-talk, and eventually, her defensiveness dissipated.

PRO TIP

Self-management—a cornerstone of emotional intelligence[18]—can help you resist the urge to react to strong emotions. Self-management is the ability to manage one's impulses in reaction to emotional stimuli. It allows for discernment between reacting instantaneously and responding with measured consideration. As Viktor Frankl described it, "Between stimulus and response there is a space. In that space is our power to choose our response. In our response lies our growth and our freedom."

Don't underestimate how hard this can be. We cannot control our emotions. We can only control what we do with them, so cultivating self-management skills is essential to emotionally intelligent leadership.

In Nobel Prize-winning economist Daniel Kahneman's book *Thinking, Fast and Slow*, he describes two modes of thought: System 1 and System 2.[19] System 1 is fast, emotional, and instinctive. System 2 is slower, more logical, and deliberative. Here's the rub: System 1 has the upper hand, so much so that it underlies our rational thoughts. When we get triggered, we react emotionally (System 1), and then we use System 2 to make sense of, or even justify, our System 1 reaction. Although we use logic to reason ourselves toward a decision, our actual decision-making

---

18 Read more about emotional intelligence (also called EQ or EI) later in this chapter.
19 Daniel Kahneman, Thinking, Fast and Slow, (New York: Farrar, Straus and Giroux. 2013).

is ruled by emotion.[20]

The simplest way to self-manage is to bring your focus to your breathing. Navy SEALs are trained[21] to use their physiology to change their psychology by practicing "box breathing"—inhale for four seconds, pause for four seconds, exhale for four seconds, and pause for four seconds.[22] Repeat. A few minutes of attention on your breath can help regulate your nervous system and disrupt the accelerated production of the stress hormones, cortisol and adrenaline, that fuel our conditioned reactions to feeling unsafe.

Granted, mindful breathing is challenging during a heated argument, but buying yourself five seconds by reaching for a glass of water can help, even if you don't drink the water. If you need more time, step away for a few minutes, center yourself, and return to the discussion afresh. Even better, reconvene a day or more later, when both/all parties are calmer. Give your body time for the stress hormones to subside so you can regain access to your brain's executive functions. When you retrain yourself to respond rather than react, "anger becomes clarity and resolve, sadness leads to compassion, jealousy becomes fuel for change,"[23] increasing your chances for a better outcome.

Given the heightened emotion in family businesses (remember the crossroads of love and money) and the lack of filter we often have with family members, developing good self-management skills can prove enormously helpful. So can

---

20 "Antonio Damasio," Wikipedia, accessed March 2, 2024, https://en.wikipedia.org/wiki/Antonio_Damasio.
21 Mar Divine, "The Breathing Technique a Navy SEAL Uses to Stay Calm and Focused," *TIME*, May 4, 2016, https://time.com/4316151/breathing-technique-navy-seal-calm-focused.
22 Melody Wilding, "Beat Stress Like a Navy SEAL With This Ridiculously Easy Exercise," *Inc.*, July 19, 2017, https://www.inc.com/melody-wilding/beat-stress-like-a-navy-seal-with-this-ridiculousl.html.
23 Diane Musho Hamilton, "Calming Your Brain During Conflict," *Harvard Business Review*, December 22, 2015, https://hbr.org/2015/12/calming-your-brain-during-conflict.

simply accepting what is. As Byron Katie says, "When you argue with reality, you lose, but only 100% of the time."[24]

BOTTOM LINE: TO LIVE A MORE PEACEFUL EXISTENCE AND ENRICH YOUR RELATIONSHIPS, CONTINUOUSLY DEVELOP YOUR SELF-MANAGEMENT SKILLS

When you receive developmental feedback using the family mindset from a boss/parent, remember that you aren't necessarily letting your parent down. Andre, a fifty-nine-year-old G2 CEO, found himself trying to over-please his father early in his career. No matter how well Andre performed, he never could satisfy his father. "If I got a $5,000 order, Dad would ask why not $8,000?" said Andre. "He just couldn't be satisfied. Now, Dad is ninety-four, and we look back and laugh, but at the time, it was very hurtful." His dad was just pushing for more, a strategy he used with many employees, not just Andre.

Remember Paula? The CEO whose mother removed the shower stalls? In a generational reversal, her mom felt hurt by Paula's feedback too. "When I became CEO, my mother had no control, and she took things very personally if I didn't invite her to an insurance meeting, for example," claimed Paula. "She heard it to mean that I didn't care, that all those years Mom led the company didn't matter."

Parents can have fragile egos too. "Even my father got defensive when I took over. I asked a question about an item on the cash flow statement, and my father snapped, 'I think we've run this company just fine so far. What do you think? That we're not good enough?'" One family member speaks using the business mindset. The other listens with the family mindset. Both are disappointed because their expectations weren't met.

---

24 "Byron Katie > Quotes > Quotable Quote," *goodreads*, accessed March 2, 2024, https://www.goodreads.com/quotes/132449-when-you-argue-with-reality-you-lose-but-only-100.

Reflecting on my own stint leading my father's business, I am sure I made my father feel marginalized and irrelevant too. My goal was to turn the company around despite him, not with him. To be truthful, I involved him only when necessary, not because I wanted his input. Looking back at my behavior from his perspective, I probably came across as cocky—not very emotionally intelligent.

In a Family Business, It's Lonely at the . . . Everywhere

In a family business, "it's lonely at the top" takes on a new meaning. When I worked for my father, I couldn't lean on family to support me when work got hard because it was family that made it hard.

Early on, I complained about my father to my brother (building factions is common in a family business). "Can you believe it?" I moaned to my brother. "He sent my report back insisting on fourteen-point font and one-and-a-half-inch margins instead of twelve-point font and one-inch margins. What a colossal waste of time." I quickly learned that complaining wasn't helpful to me or my family. Spewing my frustrations onto my brother simply created tension between my brother and our father. I had to learn how to manage my own frustration and work through my disagreements directly—not play politics using family members as pawns.

Spencer, a thirty-seven-year-old G3 leader, struggled with this too. "Where do you go for support?" he lamented. "Ultimately, the people you are closest with are the ones you are most frustrated with. You can't vent to employees. It's hard to talk with friends. A lot got compartmentalized. It was very tough to deal with." *In the work domain, family is not a sanctuary, and in the family domain, work is not an escape.* As a result, family business leadership can feel especially lonely.

PRO TIP

Emotional intelligence is the ability to identify, assess, and manage the emotions of oneself and others. Made famous by Daniel Goleman in his seminal book *Emotional Intelligence: Why It Can Matter More Than IQ*, he describes how IQ alone isn't an indicator of superior leadership effectiveness.[25] Studies show that EQ (a.k.a. EI) is the single biggest predictor of superior performance—90 percent of top performers rank high in relational skills. "When emotional intelligence was first discovered, it served as the missing link in a peculiar finding: people with the highest levels of intelligence (IQ) outperform those with average IQs just 20 percent of the time, while people with average IQs outperform those with high IQs 70 percent of the time." [26]

Unlike IQ, which is fixed for life, emotional intelligence can be developed, and it's worth it. In a 2022 article,[27] *Forbes* cites a study that calculated the ROI of emotional intelligence training to be nearly 1,500 percent. Further, studies showed that leaders with high emotional intelligence have 400 percent higher retention rates, their employees feel 50 percent more inspired by their work, productivity improves by 40 percent, and lost-time accidents decrease by 50 percent. Last, in a study[28] by Marc Brackett, whereas employees working for supervisors who scored high on EQ tests felt inspired 75 percent of the

---

25   Daniel Goleman, *Emotional Intelligence: Why It Can Matter More Than IQ*, (New York: Random House, 2005).

26   Travis Bradberry and Jean Greaves, *Emotional Intelligence 2.0* (San Diego: TalentSmart, 2009), 7-8.

27   Alex Argianas, "Adopting Emotional Intelligence In The Workplace Is More Than A 'Nice To Have,'" *Forbes*, May 4, 2022, https://www.forbes.com/sites/forbesbusinesscouncil/2022/05/04/adopting-emotional-intelligence-in-the-workplace-is-more-than-a-nice-to-have.

28   Brackett is the founding director of the Yale Center for Emotional Intelligence. The study's results are described in David Brooks, *How to Know a Person: The Art of Seeing Others Deeply and Being Deeply Seen*, (New York: Random House, 2023) 157.

time, employees working for supervisors who scored low felt inspired 25 percent of the time. The data supporting the value of developing our EQ seems endless.

The heightened emotional intensity of family business makes developing emotional intelligence especially important. As much as leaders who discount emotions in favor of reason limit their leadership effectiveness, so do leaders who discount reason in favor of emotion. The wisest, most effective leaders are those who have integrated their heads with their hearts.

BOTTOM LINE: EQ IS A GAME-CHANGER IN LEADERSHIP EFFECTIVENESS, SO CONTINUOUSLY DEVELOP YOURS.

Questions for Chapter 2

1. When have you been impacted by domain crossover power? How did it affect trust in the relationship?
2. In what ways do you use domain crossover power within your family business? How does it serve you? How does it not? Over time, how does it impact trust in your relationships?
3. Under what conditions do you react impulsively? What is your go-to impulsive response? Fight (challenge the threat)? Flight (withdraw from the threat)? Freeze (do nothing)? Or Fawn (appease the threat)?
4. When you've been triggered, how can you recenter or put space between trigger and response?
5. What rumination tapes play in your head? After separating fact from assumption, what other stories could you craft to make those same facts make perfect sense?
6. If you feel isolated as a leader in your family business, how can you find appropriate support so you feel less alone?
7. How well-developed is your EQ? How can you cultivate it more?

"If you want the truth to stand clear before you, never be for or against. The struggle between 'for' and 'against' is the mind's worst disease."

—Sent-ts'an, circa 700 CE

CHAPTER 3
SHADOW INFLUENCERS

*A*t war for four decades, the Demoulas family has fueled the longest, most contentious, and expensive lawsuits in Massachusetts history. This is the story of Market Basket, a $5B New England grocery chain that destroyed itself due to an epic, intrafamily battle for power and control.

The saga began innocently enough. In 1954, first-generation Greek immigrant brothers George and Mike Demoulas purchased their parents' store and expanded the business into a regional chain with dozens of locations throughout Massachusetts, New Hampshire, and Maine. Seventeen years later, George died suddenly, leaving Mike as sole president.

Demoulas Family Tree (Partial)

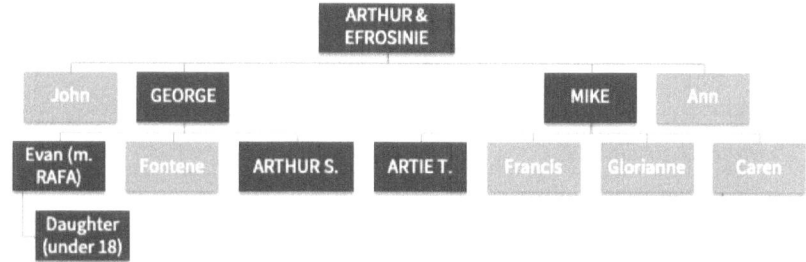

The feud began in 1989 when the Commonwealth of Massachusetts notified George's children that they owed back taxes of $1M on the shares of stock that they had sold three years earlier.

Shares they had sold? *they wondered.* But we didn't sell any shares. George's children soon discovered that Uncle Mike had been purchasing their stock, bit by bit, for over a decade.

Here's how it happened. George's kids occasionally asked Uncle Mike for money, so Uncle Mike had them sign papers, and the kids received cash. Little did they know that the papers they signed were transactions for Mike to purchase George's family shares.

Why didn't they know this? They were naïve. They trusted Uncle Mike. They didn't understand the difference between proceeds from dividends and proceeds from selling equity. They were used to getting cash when they wanted it and didn't ask questions. (Because Mike plowed every cent of profit back into the business, Market Basket didn't issue dividends at the time.)

The real drama began when two cousins, George's son Arthur and Mike's son Artie, became the lead characters in the saga. Arthur's initial lawsuit claimed Uncle Mike defrauded George's family by purchasing their stock for a fraction of its true value. That led to a countersuit of alleged wiretapping when Uncle Mike claimed to have found hidden audio devices that Arthur planted at the company headquarters.

Although Arthur was eventually cleared of that wiretapping, public drama continued with accusations of adultery, jury tampering, drug abuse, and improper contact between lawyers and judges. Two lawyers on the case were disbarred, and one day the feud devolved into a fistfight between cousins.

Finally, in 1995, the Massachusetts courts ruled in favor of George's family, and Mike had to return 43 percent of the stock (worth $206M at the time) to George's family. That left George's family with 50.5 percent ownership and Mike's family with 49.5 percent. We won control! thought Arthur.

Or so it seemed . . .

Because George died prior to 1995, the courts distributed George's shares to his descendants Evan, Fontene, and Arthur. But by then, Evan had died, leaving a young daughter who received Evan's shares in the form of a trust, whose trustee was Evan's widow, Rafa.

Arthur, concerned that an in-law could have the power to vote family shares, tried to remove Rafa as trustee and name himself as trustee instead. The nerve! thought Rafa. *So, she voted her daughter's shares in favor of the other side of the family. And because her daughter's shares amounted to more than 0.5 percent of the business, control of the business shifted back to Mike's family!*

It gets even better.

Market Basket thrived under Mike and his son Artie's leadership. By 2008, Artie was president and CEO, and he inspired devoted followers among customers and employees alike. For example, when the profit-sharing plan lost $46M in one quarter during the 2008 financial crisis, Artie insisted that the company make up the loss. This filled his employees with relief and gratitude but enraged Arthur, who argued, "Artie is enriching employees at the expense of the family!"

Arthur objected to Artie's strategy of reinvesting instead of harvesting profits. From his board seat, Arthur moved to extract a few hundred million in cash from the business by cutting employee benefits, lowering wages, raising prices, and delaying capital investments.

Artie countered that good wages and benefits paired with low prices were a competitive advantage that fueled customer and employee loyalty. Without it, Market Basket would lose its differentiation in the marketplace, thereby decimating the potential for better investment returns for future generations of the Demoulas family.

Artie thought, After receiving $500M in dividends already, Arthur is just greedy for wanting more. *With 50.5 percent control, Artie voted against more dividends for Arthur's family.*

Instead, Artie announced a 4 percent price discount throughout the stores, saying that his customers needed the money more than his family did. He was hailed as a George Bailey in It's a Wonderful Life *for his* willingness to put people over profit, and he became known by customers and employees as "our Artie."

But Arthur wasn't the only family member frustrated by the limited access to cash. Rafa, as trustee for her daughter, wanted access to some cash too. So, in the summer of 2013, Rafa shifted her allegiance from Artie to Arthur, and Arthur regained control of the business. Within the next year, the board of directors ousted Artie as CEO.

The market immediately revolted.

With decades of loyal tenure under Artie's leadership, the executive team objected to Arthur's coup and initiated a walkout that crippled the company for weeks. Eight top corporate managers resigned. Shoppers boycotted the stores. Suppliers slowed down deliveries. Shelves were empty, and Market Basket lost close to 90 percent of its business during the next six weeks. That's over $10M a day! Customers and employees banded together to hold rallies reminiscent of rock festivals, with music and beach balls and people carrying signs demanding Artie return as president.

Two months after Artie was terminated, he, with the help of private equity investors, purchased George's family's shares for $1.6B, and Artie was reinstated as CEO. Market Basket was back in business.

But in 2016, Arthur filed new lawsuits demanding information related to an IRS audit. The saga continues . . .

◆ ◆ ◆

A true story,[29] this byzantine drama is an extreme example of how power struggles can manifest in family businesses. Both Artie and Arthur used the tools of the business mindset (courts, trusts, ownership shares) to defend their beliefs from the family mindset (fairness). Interestingly, the real power resided with a shadow influencer, Rafa, who was not born into the family, owned zero shares, and never worked in the business. An oft-hidden yet potent force in a family business, shadow

---

29 Credit for story detail goes to *The Boston Globe*, which has covered this family saga for decades.

influencers can have disproportionate sway, despite having no formal power, authority, or even role in the business. As the Demoulas family experienced, shadow influencers can dramatically change outcomes.

Although shadow influence can be remarkably helpful in a family business, let's begin with how shadow influence can lead to confusion and frustration.

Stakeholders Aren't Always Shareholders

At fifty-three, Aaron still deferred to his mom's wishes when it came to tough CEO decisions. She had no formal part in the family business (her husband had founded the regional HVAC installation business) but insisted that Aaron employ his brother-in-law, Frank. Aaron strongly objected. "He's a huge problem," claimed Aaron. "Frank likes the respect of being a manager and owner but doesn't come to meetings, and he doesn't manage."

Aaron thought creatively about how to get out of this situation. He tried to buy Frank out, then tried to sell the business entirely, but his mother couldn't bear the thought of her daughter's husband looking for work in his fifties. She *insisted* Aaron employ him. Aaron said, "I couldn't get out of the business because my mother kept pleading 'shalom bayit,'" a Yiddish expression meaning *peace in the home*. "When we struggle, Mom says, 'It's family. Work it out. Work it out.' So, a compromise is always made."

Aaron, preferring the business mindset, sought to lead an organizationally healthy and efficient business. Aaron's mom, leaning into the family mindset, sought to care for and protect her daughter by insisting that Frank retain his employment. In Aaron's case, the family mindset norm of "obey your parents" prevailed.

In a public company, mothers have no power, and it's absurd to think that they could. Conversely, in a family business, mothers can wield a fierce Mama Bear power to protect even their adult children, *especially* children whom she fears are less able to care for themselves. (Papa bears do this too.)

Ironically, this protective instinct can preordain a parent's worst fears. When parents shield their children from failure, the children struggle to develop the life skills and confidence to thrive on their own. They remain dependent on others, which ultimately makes them vulnerable, not safe.

After decades of protecting her daughter by demanding that Aaron employ Frank, Frank had no confidence that he could work outside the business. By the time he turned fifty, everyone assumed it was too late to start. Framed as a support :: challenge polarity, Aaron's family overfocused on support and under-focused on challenge.

Parental Protection Doesn't Last Forever

The loss of a shadow influencer can upend the status quo of a family business. Shadow influencers often foster stability and consistency in the family, so when they depart, the remaining family members are left to renegotiate power. It is often a period of great anxiety in the family and business.

Alessandra, forty-five-year-old G3 CEO of her family's business, fears what will happen when her parents die. Although her father actively supports her as leader of the business, her siblings actively do not. "If I didn't have my dad behind me, it'd be horrible. I don't know what I'd do," she exclaims. "My parents work hard to keep the family together. If they weren't so strong, my siblings would be fully estranged. They just want their money. I'm not sure what will happen after my parents pass." Alessandra's parents are the linchpin to harmony in their family, so when they pass, tension is likely to rise while the new power structure settles into place.

PRO TIP

The first cornerstone of emotional intelligence is self-awareness, which has two components. The first is the ability to know, *in the moment*, when you are being triggered by a strong emotion. The second is knowing how others perceive you. Self-awareness is the critical first step of emotional intelligence because, without self-awareness, our emotions have us—we don't have our emotions.

Although self-awareness doesn't require decades of therapy, it does necessitate self-inquiry—a willingness to take an honest look inside to develop "a straightforward and honest understanding of what makes you tick. People in high self-awareness are remarkably clear in their understanding of what they do well, what motivates and satisfies them, and which people and situations push their buttons."[30]

The quickest and most effective way to improve awareness of your triggers (or any emotion) is to shift attention to your body. Our bodies reflect our emotions in the form of physical sensations such as increased heartbeat, heat on the neck, weight on the chest, etc. Why the body? Our bodies don't lie. Our brains easily convince us of what we want to be true, but our bodies reflect our actual truth.

When you notice a shift of sensation in your body, get curious. Resist the urge to react (unless you are in immediate danger). Instead, sit with the sensation and notice how it changes or doesn't change. As you observe yourself, notice your emotions with curiosity, not judgment. This is important because if you observe with judgment—"There I go again!"—you exacerbate the emotionality, which hinders effective decision-making. Not helpful. Be kind to yourself and simply observe with neutrality. Give yourself permission to be imperfect. We all are.

Another strategy for self-awareness is to imagine you are on the balcony of a dancehall, observing yourself on the dance floor (or maybe you are observing yourself as a juggler from the stands circus . . . find a metaphor that works for you). Gaining distance from the emotion helps you observe without judgment. Emotions

---

30   *Emotional Intelligence 2.0* by Travis Bradberry and Jean Greaves, (San Diego: TalentSmart, 2009), 25.

aren't inherently good or bad. They are simply body sensations that serve a useful purpose. Emotions are signposts[31] of something you need or value to help you make good choices.

The last strategy I offer to enhance self-awareness leverages modern technology, an app. With the help of a *Mood Meter*, the How We Feel app helps you "gain greater insight around the causes and consequences of your feelings and learn research-based strategies to help you regulate your feelings to achieve greater well-being."[32]

The second aspect of self-awareness is knowing how others perceive you. Your friends and family can point out your reactive tendencies under stress, and feedback surveys can provide enlightening data too.

Don't get hung up on what is "the truth." Just because people perceive you as arrogant, for example, doesn't mean you see yourself that way. But what a gift to learn that your behaviors leave others with that impression. When feedback does sting, ask yourself what part of the judgment is true so you can learn from it. What part of the judgment is not true? You can ignore it. Early in one's career, feedback tends to sting, but eventually, most leaders learn to value feedback as a gift.

BOTTOM LINE: EFFECTIVE EQ STARTS WITH EFFECTIVE SELF-AWARENESS.

Married-Ins as Shadow Influencers

Parents aren't the only power players. Spouses who marry into a family business can also wield substantial influence. When Nancy (age forty-eight) married Jeff (age fifty-eight), his oldest child, Max

---

31 *Emotional Agility: Get Unstuck, Embrace Change, and Thrive in Work and Life* by Susan David (New York: Avery, 2016), 117 and 210.
32 "How We Feel App," accessed March 2, 2024, https://marcbrackett.com/mood-meter-app.

(age thirty-six), had already joined the law firm his dad founded, but Nancy wanted Max *out*, so she pressured Jeff to fire his son.

Here's Nancy's perspective.

I got married pretty young, and soon after I gave birth to my third child, my marriage fell apart. For years, I focused on providing for my children. Then I met Jeff, a successful entrepreneur who was divorced. He is the love of my life! He welcomed us into his world, and we were so happy . . . until I met his son, Max.

Max joined the law firm after earning his law degree at Yale, but he thinks he's better than me because I didn't get accepted to Yale when I applied. Max didn't even greet my son at the company picnic last month! He pretends to be nice to my face, but he is fake.

When Max refused to invite my kids to his son's briss, I raised a stink with Jeff. My kids aren't good enough for him? I told Jeff that one of us had to go, and it wasn't going to be me. Not one employee at this firm could treat me, the wife of the founder, with such disrespect. He doesn't live this firm's values or deserve to work here. Jeff needs to teach Max a lesson and fire him.

Here's Jeff's perspective.

I started my law firm two years before the birth of my first child, and my biggest mistake was putting all my energy into my work. Although the firm is thriving, it came at the price of my marriage, and I'm now divorced from the mother of my children.

A few years ago, I met Nancy, the love of my life. She means everything to me! She is my top priority, and I'll never put work ahead of family ever again.

But she and my son Max have locked horns in an epic battle of wills. This standoff is wreaking havoc on my marriage and destroying my relationship with Max. I told Max that he needs to accept Nancy into his life and make peace. Until he does, he will not advance at this company, no matter how talented he is.

I love both my wife and my son fiercely, but they are ripping me apart.

And here's Max's perspective.

When I grew up, my dad was never around. All he cared about was his law firm. So, I worked my tail off in school and completed a law degree so I could get a seat at the table that mattered most to him: the firm.

But when I got there, all the rules had changed. He didn't care about the firm anymore. All he cared about was Nancy and his new family. Worse, he's the dad to her kids that I always wanted him to be for me.

During my son's briss, for just one day, I wanted my dad to be there for me. I couldn't bear the thought of my father focusing on Nancy's kids during this sacred event. That's why I didn't invite them.

Lately, I can't do anything right with Nancy. Yesterday, Dad lectured me for ten minutes because I didn't say hi to Nancy's son at the company picnic. I didn't even see him there! It's just crazy. My dad told me I wouldn't progress in my career until I made up with Nancy. I don't know how! I am so frustrated.

Shadow influencers can leave you confounded when you cannot see the full picture—they often operate in the shadows. Feeling hurt, rejected, and eager to make that pain go away, Nancy lobbied for Jeff to fire Max, but Max didn't know that his job was at risk. All Max knew was that he would be demoted until he made nice with Nancy.

PRO TIP

Notice how each character in this drama is deeply entrenched in their individual story. Although each story draws from the same set of facts, each story is quite different, and each character is an innocent lamb in their story. That's how our own stories work.

Humans are wired for story.[33] It's how we make sense of the

---

[33] Jonathan Gottschall, *The Storytelling Animal: How Stories Make Us Human*, (New York: HarperCollins Publishers, 2013).

buzzing confusion of events in our lives. However, the stories we craft aren't "the truth." They are the storyteller's truth. When we see undeniable facts, we craft a story that brings coherence to the facts.

For example, Nancy and Max used the same fact (Max didn't greet Nancy's son at the picnic), but they told very different stories about the fact. Each story made perfect sense to the storyteller, but each storyteller filled in the gaps between facts with assumptions, opinions, and judgments.

Here's what's risky about stories: The more we ruminate about them, they more they become entrenched. The neural pathways in our brains grow stronger with each repetition until they feel like undeniable truths.

So, when someone triggers you, ask what story you are telling yourself about that person. Specify the facts of the story (*she rolled her eyes*) and the assumptions in the story (*she thinks I'm stupid*). Most family members are exceptionally adept at reading other family members' micro-expressions, which makes it tempting to draw conclusions from nonverbal cues, whether accurate or not. We humans are masterful storytellers.

Once you have separated facts from assumptions, craft some different stories that make equally perfect sense of the facts. For example, *She left her tax return on the copy machine*, or *Her client canceled lunch again*. Notice which story sources its fuel from your fears and insecurities. Once you have multiple stories, determine if you need to know the other person's perspective. If you don't, let it go. If you do, read chapter 6 to learn how to have brave conversations.

Emotionally intelligent leaders recognize when they are telling themselves a story. They separate facts from assumptions and check their assumptions before drawing conclusions.

BOTTOM LINE: CATCH YOURSELF IN YOUR STORIES BEFORE THEY BECOME YOUR TRUTH.

Two events laid the path for reconciliation in this family. First, Nancy, Jeff, and Max met and shared their respective stories with each other. With conscious effort (and the aid of a nonfamily facilitator), each person found empathy for the other people's perspectives. They didn't agree that the other stories were "right," but they were able to empathize with their emotional pain.

Next, they crafted a shared story. The new story was more comprehensive, nuanced, and included elements of each person's original story. Nancy and Max met alone for a long lunch. As they slowly let their respective guards down, they found a shared childhood experience... both had lost a sibling when they were teens. With empathy as a foundation, they started the journey of building mutual trust.

That is social awareness, another cornerstone of emotional intelligence, in action. They learned to see the world through someone else's eyes, and today, they coexist in relative harmony.

Blindsiding Shadow Influence

Bibi, a forty-five-year-old nonfamily COO, never knew the real reason he lost his job. When he opened his email Monday morning, he was shocked to read the announcement that Francie, his boss and CEO, had just promoted her thirty-two-year-old son to be president. Although a solid performer, her son wasn't ready to be president.

Bibi was livid. First, as a member of the executive team, how was he not informed before the company-wide announcement? Worse, why wasn't Bibi considered for the role? He'd been with the company for twenty years and believed he was in line for the president role. When he discussed it with Francie, he got the brush-off, which just angered him more. To top it off, Bibi now reported to Francie's thirty-two-year-old son.

Little did Bibi know the real reason for the son's promotion. Francie wanted to hire a talented VP of supply chain who was in recovery from substance abuse, behavior that alarmed Francie's husband. Sensitive to his wife's private struggles with addiction, Francie's husband surreptitiously yet unambiguously insisted that this new VP *not* report to his wife. After much discussion, the family promoted their son to president prematurely to put a reporting layer between CEO and VP, thus distancing the two from each other.

Unable to overcome feelings of disrespect, Bibi had a chip on his shoulder from then on, and it showed up in his attitude at work. Within six months, Francie's son terminated Bibi's employment, and Bibi never knew what hit him. That's how shadow influence can work in a family business. Married-ins—without a role in the business—can impact the business system in unknowable ways.

PRO TIP

Shadow influencers can be deft users of soft power (sometimes *power with* or *shared power*) by appealing to intangibles such as fairness and shared values to engender cooperation. At its best, soft power influences behind the scenes for the greater good. At its worst, soft power leverages relationships to achieve overly self-oriented goals, destructive to the greater good.

Because this power dynamic often operates in the shadows, it can be difficult to know when you are impacted by it. Here are some strategies to increase your sensitivity to it.

When something just doesn't feel right, observe the "system" by watching how it responds to change. Like a mobile that hangs from the ceiling, changing one element of a system impacts the rest of the system, so observe how the system functions and pay special attention to behavior anomalies that don't seem to have a cause.

Behavior in a system tends to settle into reliable, repeatable patterns until there are changes, such as new entrants (marriages, children), exits (deaths, divorces), or a part of the system behaves differently. When you notice a disruption to the normal patterns, look for activity that took place prior to these new patterns and get curious.

As you sense into the system, action your curiosity by asking direct questions. That doesn't mean accusing anyone of anything; it simply means bringing heartfelt curiosity to relevant relationships. If you uncover new information, notice if you get triggered (your body sensations will inform you), and pause before choosing a response.

Last, when you do choose to act, conduct micro-experiments within the system and notice what does or does not happen. Continue these micro-experiments until you are satisfied that you have learned as much as you can learn.[34]

Soft power is influence—the ability to achieve objectives without threat or force. An essential leadership skill in any business, it's critical in a family business, given the unorthodox power dynamics in play. Here are some resources[35] to enhance influencing skills: *Never Split the Difference* by Chris Voss & Tahl Raz, *How to Win Friends and Influence People* by Dale Carnegie, *The Culture Code* by Daniel Coyle, *You Have More Influence Than You Think* by Vanessa Bohns, and Harvard Business Review's *Influence and Persuasion* in HBR's Emotional Intelligence Series.

In *Family Champions and Champion Families*,[36] Joshua Nacht describes the role of the family champion as the family owner who engages and inspires the family to work collaboratively. Skilled at

---

34 This borrows gently from Otto Sharmer, *Theory U: Leading from the Future as It Emerges*, (Oakland: Berrett-Koehler Publishers, 2016).

35 Two more: Rebecca Knight, "How to Increase Your Influence at Work," *Harvard Business Review*, February 16, 2018,.https://hbr.org/2018/02/how-to-increase-your-influence-at-work. and Caroline Castrillion, "How To Build Influence Without Authority At Work," *Forbes*, September 24, 2023, https://www.forbes.com/sites/carolinecastrillon/2023/09/24/how-to-build-influence-without-authority-at-work.

36 Joshua Nacht, *Family Champions and Champion Families: Developing Family Leaders to Sustain the Family Enterprise*. (Chicago: The Family Business Consulting Group. 2018.)

using soft power to forge agreements, family champions provide the essential glue needed to sustain family cohesion.

Although adolescents tend to favor manipulation and coercion to get their needs met, many adults learn to replace "power over" with "power with." "Power with" is shared power built on respect, empowerment, and collaborative decision-making. It can help build bridges within groups and across differences, thereby facilitating collective action.[37] Building trusting relationships is crucial because, in the absence of trust, we tend to revert to coercive "power over" to get our needs met.

BOTTOM LINE: SHADOW INFLUENCE IS AN INVISIBLE YET POTENT FORCE IN FAMILY BUSINESSES.

Shadow Influencers as a Force for Good

Shadow influence can help keep a family business focused, as Calvin, a forty-three-year-old G4 CEO, learned. One of six brothers raised by the same parents, Calvin and his siblings grew up absorbing their parents' worldview, unlike their cousin Wade, who grew up influenced by a different set of parents. Wade brings a more objective lens to Calvin and his brothers' shenanigans. "Although my cousin subscribes to the same foundational values we all subscribe to, he brings something to the table that we cannot," admires Calvin. "The six of us can trigger childhood stuff by simply the tone in our voice. Wade is more objective; he doesn't have the same emotional connection. He can shoot a straighter arrow, which keeps us on task." Thanks to the influence of a different set of parents, Wade calms and stabilizes the business.

Whether positive or negative, shadow influencers wield great

---

37 Graeme Stuart, "4 types of power: What are power over; power with; power to and power within?" accessed March 2, 2024, https://sustainingcommunity.wordpress.com/2019/02/01/4-types-of-power.

power in family business due to the presence of the family mindset. This can be quite frustrating to employees (and advisers) who expect only the business mindset. Understanding the presence of the family mindset explains why shadow influencers have so much sway.

Questions for Chapter 3

1. Who are the shadow influencers in your family business?
2. What motivates these shadow influencers? How can you find out if you don't know?
3. What relationship do you have (want to have, need to have) with these shadow influencers?
4. How can you use your influence to advocate for your needs? For the greater good?
5. If you don't like the feedback you've received, what's at risk for you by hearing what others think?
6. What stories do you have that could use some discernment between facts and assumptions?
7. How might another person's story feel challenging for them, even if it wouldn't feel the same for you?
8. If trust is low in your family business, how can you (re)build it? What are your options if you don't?

"Life is strong and fragile. It's a paradox . . . It's both things, like quantum physics: It's a particle and a wave at the same time. It all exists all together."

—Joan Jett

CHAPTER 4
UNORTHODOX POWER

"*L*ooking back," said Genevieve, "I should've seen it coming."
On the eve of his sixtieth birthday, her father, Dantrell, gathered his four children in the dining room. The youngest, Genevieve, recalls how he kept shifting around in his chair. That's not like him, *she thought.*

Her father began. "I've engaged a family business consultant to help me determine which one of the four of you will succeed me as CEO when I step down." The CEO role was no small job—Dantrell had grown the business to $3B in annual revenue. "I want an experienced consultant to make this recommendation, not me," he continued. "I love you all so much, and I don't want to choose between you, but I do want only one of you in that role."

All four sisters sucked in their breath as they caught each other's glances. Each held a different role in the business their grandfather had started, and they'd been wondering about succession for years. Finally, there was movement!

After two years of analysis and discussion, Dantrell reunited his daughters in the dining room and announced that Genevieve, the thirty-six-year-old and youngest sister, would succeed him as CEO. This time, the only sound was the ticktock of the grandfather clock while Genevieve *looked directly at her father. She already knew the news.*

The announcement hit Abigail, Genevieve's oldest sister, the hardest. It brought Abigail right back to high school when their parents nagged her about her grades and grounded her on weekends. Genevieve always had it easier, *thought Abigail.* Smart, pretty, and popular, Genevieve easily maintained a 4.0 GPA, and she had no curfew. It wasn't fair.

A few months later, Dantrell updated the shareholder agreement to allow for phantom stock for a key employee. When he asked his daughters to sign it, Abigail refused. She found different reasons every time, but she brought the process to a standstill for over nine months.

Fearing she'd lose key employees if the new shareholder agreement wasn't signed, Genevieve grew furious. Abigail's obstructionist behavior is putting this business at risk! *Genevieve thought about raising the issue to the board of directors, but why bother? The board consisted of herself, her father, and her older sisters.*

"This feels so circular," complained Genevieve. "My sisters report to me, but they are also board members, so I report to them. If I burn out as CEO, it's not going to be because of the work; it's going to be because of the stress of managing the relationships with my sisters."

◆ ◆ ◆

Power in a family business doesn't follow traditional business norms. It can be confusing, circular, and frustrating due to the conflicting norms of the family mindset and business mindset.

The youngest of four sisters, Genevieve represented the bottom of the sibling hierarchy yet a generational peer with her sisters. The family system was stable until her father announced that Genevieve would succeed him. That hierarchy change led to a renegotiation of power in the business domain and a disruption to the stability in the family domain. It took several years for relationship stability to resettle, as each sister grappled with the power change in her own way.

Sibling groups have both equality *and* hierarchy built into them.

Although siblings are considered equal members of a generation,[38] birth order gives rise to a natural hierarchy within it. When the lowest rank in the sibling hierarchy became the highest rank in the professional hierarchy, *both* the equality and hierarchy norms of the family mindset were upended.

Some families manage this better than others. As CEO, Calvin (G4 from chapter 3) reported to the board, which was made up of his parents, uncles, and aunts. However, many of those same relatives reported to him as employees. Fortunately for Calvin and his family, they are conscious about their respective roles at any moment. "G3 sits on the board, and I submit to the board," says Calvin. "I work for them, even though some of them work for me as CEO. We're all in it together. We respect our roles and responsibility boundaries." Calvin's family manages the tension between the family mindset and business mindset quite well.

Who Makes the Decisions Around Here?

Genevieve's story also exemplifies a confusing phenomenon in family businesses: power is distributed in atypical ways, making decision authority muddy. Decision authority in public companies is clearer. Employees of public companies report to managers, who report to leaders, who report to a board whose fiduciary duty is to represent the interests of the thousands of (mostly anonymous) shareholders. Decision authority is clear and hierarchical.[39]

By contrast, shareholders in a private family business are much fewer in number, and everyone usually knows who they are. More importantly, family *employees* are also often *owners* of the business, sometimes even when they are teenagers sweeping floors in the warehouse. This can befuddle nonfamily employees.

Alicia loved her job as president of a family business—until the

---

38   Generational equality and fairness can become more complex in blended families and families with half-siblings.
39   Most businesses operate hierarchically, but not all, such as those in a holacracy.

reorg. She reported to the CEO, Joseph, and after the reorg, Joseph's brother Steve started reporting to her.

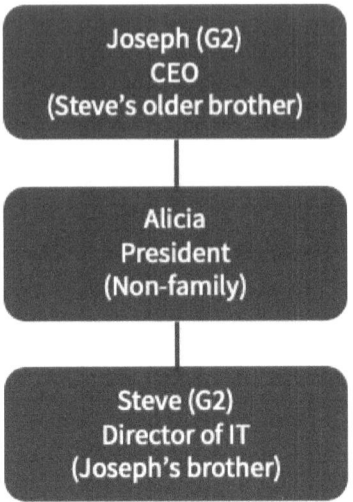

It started out well. Steve was a talented IT director, but Alicia didn't know how to respond when, in his one-on-one with Alicia, Steve insisted that she replace the director of marketing. As an IT director, Steve was way outside of his lane. But as an owner? Did he have the authority to direct her behavior? Confused and irritated, she raised the situation to her boss, Joseph.

Fortunately, Joseph understood why Steve behaved the way he did. The norms of the family (owner) mindset conflicted with the norms of the business mindset, leaving Steve unclear about when and how to raise his concerns. With this awareness, Joseph, Alicia, and Steve met to clarify governance expectations. They agreed that going forward, ownership discussions take place in ownership meetings, business discussions take place in business meetings, and family discussions take place in family meetings. Clear governance protocols in a family business play an important role in supporting both the family and the business. (Learn more about family business governance in chapter 8.)

PRO TIP

Family members who work in a family business operate in a fishbowl because what family says as a whisper, nonfamily hears as a shout. If you are a family employee, stay mindful of what you do and say because nonfamily employees tend to overanalyze your words and deeds.

Modern Families Add Complexity

Modern families can produce unorthodox distributions of power. Amos (age sixty-two, CEO of his family office) acknowledges his circumstances are "like *The Jerry Springer Show*." When he hosted his son's wedding to Yasmin, he met Yasmin's younger sister, Zasha, and they started dating. Four years later, Amos married Zasha (yes, his daughter-in-law's younger sister. You cannot make this up!)

Although Yasmin worked in the family office, Zasha (Yasmin's younger sister *and now stepmother!*) had an "in" with the boss and frequently convinced Amos to override Yasmin's decisions. What a confluence of sibling rivalry, shadow influencers, domain crossover, and unorthodox power all at once. Throw traditional decision authority out the window with these family dynamics!

Blocking Power

Remember Abigail from this chapter's opening story? She demonstrated a subtle yet potent form of power in family businesses: blocking power.[40] Unlike hard power from domain crossover or soft power from shadow influencers, blocking power halts progress. With unresolved resentment from childhood, Abigail prevented the update to the shareholders' agreement by refusing to sign.

---

40   Credit for the concept of blocking power goes to Matthew Wesley, https://www.thewesleygroup.com/blog, who built upon the concept of soft power and hard power from Joseph Nye's, *Bound To Lead: The Changing Nature Of American Power*, (New York: Basic Books, 1991).

Blocking power can show up in a few ways. In addition to active opposition, as in Abigail's example, blocking power can also show up as passive sabotage, such as raising ever more questions about a document that's been discussed, negotiated, and renegotiated for months.

Sometimes blocking power lasts for generations. Fred and Thomas fought incessantly as kids, so when their father died in 1942, each inherited a different business. Then in 1963, Thomas needed a cash infusion, so he asked Fred for a loan. Fred lent Thomas the cash, and Thomas pledged 50 percent of the stock of his business to Fred as collateral for the loan.

A few years later, Thomas repaid the loan plus interest, but Fred simply refused to return his brother's equity. Fred's use of blocking power deepened the divide between brothers until, eventually, Fred died, and Fred's children inherited 50 percent of their Uncle Thomas's business. This violated the family mindset of fairness, and both sides of the family knew it.

Over the next two decades, both families continued to operate, but their results were quite different. While Thomas's business grew significantly, Fred's business collapsed from industry deregulation. Fortunately, Fred's descendants found good jobs elsewhere.

Still, Fred's descendants owned 50 percent of Thomas's business.

Fred's children knew that their 50 percent ownership of Uncle Thomas's business wasn't "fair," and they certainly hadn't contributed to its growth in value. So, in 1985, Fred's descendants sold their 50 percent stake back to Thomas's family for one dollar.

As Thomas's son describes it, "What a win-win. The key to success has been communication with my cousin. We get along and communicate really well. We trust and respect each other impeccably. We each represent the two sides: Fred and Dad. My side of the family trusts me, his side trusts him, and we trust each other. But it took a generation to get there." When later generations are less emotionally triggered by historical events, they can bring a more objective lens to the past and right the wrongs of history.

Fairness Is Subjective

What's fair to one person may not feel fair to another. Take James, age sixty-four, G2 chairman who married into a family business forty-five years ago. His father-in-law bypassed his own son in favor of James to be CEO. Raw from his father's rejection, the son's emotional injury played out in the next generation.

James successfully grew the business for forty years and eventually convinced his son Louis to join the company. The only G3 to work in the business, Louis knew to start at the bottom to earn credibility as a future leader.

However, ten years into his family business career, Louis's cousins blocked his advancement at every turn. They objected to Louis's promotions and his seat on the board because his cousins never forgave Louis's father, an *in-law*, for being chosen over their dad. It wasn't "fair." Louis is convinced he is paying the price for his grandfather's decision, four decades earlier, to choose an in-law over a biological son.

Given these unorthodox power dynamics in family businesses, it's helpful to remember that sometimes "it's not about you." In other words, because a family business is a dynamic system, some of which you can see and some of which you cannot, when your experiences don't make logical sense, it may be due to an unknown part of the system—sometimes a history that took place before you were born. Your leadership challenge is to rise to the occasion today, despite the cards that were dealt generations earlier.

PRO TIP

Blocking power tends to arise when the stakes are high and someone feels railroaded or unheard. Asking family members to collaboratively steward shared assets is a tall ask, given the competing priorities of each individual. That's why defining shared interests is important. It can be the glue that makes the discomfort of navigating competing priorities worthwhile.

Blocking power at its best slows down a fast-moving system,

allowing people the time to make better decisions. Blocking power at its worst forces important issues into the eddy of a river, swirling in circles endlessly.

When you are on the receiving end of blocking power, pause to assess the value in slowing down. The system may benefit from a healthy pause before resuming its normal pace. Next, get curious and listen actively. Seek to understand the genuine interests of whoever exercises blocking power and take their important needs into consideration. They may be unconsciously rebalancing the overuse of a pole in a polarity.

Many families designate a black sheep, a.k.a. a DDO (dedicated difficult one). Black sheep tend to be countercultural. "Our family is [fill in the blank], and [our black sheep] isn't like us." If your family has a DDO, ask yourself if they represent an underrepresented pole of a polarity. For example, if your family culture is agile, shoot-from-the-hip, and quick-moving, you may have a DDO who is thoughtful, methodical, and reflective. The countercultural DDO may unconsciously balance out the overuse of *fast* in your family's management of the fast :: thorough polarity.

Your family culture may be highspeed (fast), and the DDO represents reflective (thorough). Naturally, the contemplative one irritates all those who favor high speed. Yet, the family preference for high speed may lead to its overuse, such as sloppy agreements, under-vetting suppliers, and a lack of cohesive strategy. In reaction to the overuse of high speed, the DDO may swing hard to contemplative, to counterbalance energy. Often, the stronger the family's attachment to one pole (high speed), the stronger the DDO's attachment to its opposite (contemplative), which can lead to the DDO's overuse of *thorough*, such as analysis paralysis.

When your DDO is highlighting the overuse of a polarity you didn't see before, keep them close and harness their wisdom. As the African proverb goes, "The child who is not embraced by the village will burn it down to feel its warmth." Although nobody likes to feel alienated, feeling alienated by *family* cuts to the core. Belonging in the family is a human craving. Those who feel excluded tend to demonstrate destructive behavior to soothe their immediate ego needs, such as exacting revenge (fight), cutting off ties (flight), grumbling in pained silence (freeze), or pleading for acceptance (fawn). The reactive behavior of a rejected family member is often a sorrowful wail for love. Communicate clear boundaries and be kind.[41]

Sometimes simply acknowledging how someone feels (even if you don't feel the same way) can ease the urge to exercise blocking power. Ultimately, if slowing down, wholeheartedly listening, and coalescing around shared interests fail to relieve the grip of blocking power, it may be helpful to bring in a family systems therapist.[42]

BOTTOM LINE: BLOCKING POWER IS OFTEN A SIGNAL THAT SOMEONE FEELS DISREGARDED. LISTEN TO LEARN FROM THEM.

Elder Status Still Rules

The power of a matriarch or patriarch can last far beyond the years of any formal power granted by job title or ownership because the family mindset presumes deference to elders over any business mindset protocols.

Mason, a forty-five-year-old G2 CEO, spent two years negotiating with his brothers and father to change the compensation plan from equal pay to market-based pay. After two years of consultants and conversations, they settled on a plan that included a base salary and performance-based bonuses. However, at the end of the first year, when they gathered to discuss their first bonus, performance naturally differed by brother. Unable to tolerate the discomfort of conflict and inequality, their seventy-six-year-old father suddenly announced,

---

41   Under certain extreme circumstances, such as threats to one's safety, keeping some family members close is not advised.
42   I am partial to family therapists who are trained in Bowen Family Systems.

"Let's forget about the bonus structure. We'll all get the same amount." What took two years to establish using the business mindset was gone in a flash, courtesy of the family mindset.

Similarly, Henry (G3 CEO from chapter 1) witnessed this deferential power dynamic every summer when Henry's father and uncle returned from their retirement community in Arizona to the Midwest to visit family. Following their retirement ten years prior, Henry had professionalized the operations, which had desperately outgrown the ad hoc, entrepreneurial leadership style of G1 and G2. Using the business mindset, Henry established standards, processes, and a structured hierarchy for clear decision-making and empowered delegation.

But every summer, Henry's father and uncle returned to the business, and "the entire dynamic in the building changed," he said. "They had rewarded loyalty," Henry said, "so the legacy employees reverted to old behavior in an unconscious, Pavlovian manner," wreaking havoc with the organizational structure. "The old guard hated formal structure, and the culture regressed to the old communication patterns, challenging the authority of their supervisors," he claimed. Upending the tacit deference granted to the elder generation takes effort. Clear, consistent communication with all employees during and after leadership succession helps, and even then, old behavior patterns can be hard to break.

The Crux of the Tension

All three power dynamics, whether it's shadow influencers, domain crossover, or unorthodox power, can lead to conflict. The crux of the tension rests in the conflicting rules of the family mindset and the business mindset. In chapters 9 and 10, we will explore a variety of ways to manage these tensions. But first, let's explore how they manifest when integrating privileges and responsibilities (chapter 5) and fostering constructive conflict (chapter 6).

Questions for Chapter 4

1. Where are the family mindset expectations of decision-making conflicting with the business mindset expectations of decision-making?
2. Where do you see blocking power in your family business?
3. Where is power circular, and what impact does it have on the business? The family?
4. What "injustices" or "emotional injuries" from prior generations could be addressed now? How might you address them?
5. How is elder power exercised in your family business? How is it serving you? How is it not?

"What separates privilege from entitlement is gratitude."

—Brené Brown

"The more freedom we enjoy, the greater the responsibility we bear, toward others as well as ourselves."

—Oscar Arias Sánchez, Former President of Costa Rica & Nobel Peace Prize Laureate

CHAPTER 5
INTEGRATING PRIVILEGES AND RESPONSIBILITIES

"*I am living in the twilight zone,*" muttered Paulo to his husband. "*How do I do right by my family* and *do right by the business?*"

Still in his rock climbing clothes, Paulo boiled water for his tea, musing at the irony of it all. Rock climbing is supposed to be his release from pressure, but for the entire climb, he ruminated about his older sister Sofia. He'd caught Sofia in another lie. A stupid lie. An expensive lie. An unnecessary lie.

Unlike Sofia who joined their father in the family's landscaping business right out of school, Paulo went into investment banking. A decade later, their father invited Paulo into the family business.

It started small. A little lie here and there, but it soon escalated. Paulo caught Sofia asking employees to work on her home, maintain her lawn, plant her garden, all on company time, using company money. Of course, she lied about it, gaslighting anyone who challenged her. Her greatest talent seemed to be dodging responsibility and accountability.

Three years later, the tension between Paulo and Sofia was visible to employees. "I can't bring it up to Dad," he continued. "Sofia's got him wrapped around her pinky. He won't acknowledge that the employees don't respect her either." His dad refuses to take a side.

Paulo turned to face his husband, who cringed while listening to the same broken record. "I want to leave," Paulo said. "But leaving would crush Dad. He's hell-bent on passing this business on to Sofia and me, and I don't want to let him down. It's just that I can't do it anymore. I don't trust Sofia, she's a drag on the business, and I don't want to carry her load for the rest of my career," he said.

"How can I be a good brother and son and *protect the business at the same time?*"

◆ ◆ ◆

The family mindset says *be a good family member. Love unconditionally.* The business mindset says *challenge inefficiencies. Weed out the dead weight.* Paulo doesn't see a way to do both. He and Sofia live at opposite ends of a responsibilities :: privileges polarity, where Paulo leans hard toward responsibility, and Sofia leans toward privilege.

While the last three chapters explored how the family :: business polarity leads to unique power dynamics in family businesses, this chapter explores how the family :: business polarity manifests as internal pressure, frustration, and angst within individual leaders.

A word of caution. The next two chapters highlight some of the most emotionally challenging aspects of working in a family business. Not all family businesses suffer these pressures, so please don't let this book scare you away from family businesses. It's important to have your eyes open to these phenomena so you can manage these tensions effectively.

Working in family businesses can be joyful. You can cocreate something meaningful for the world, work with people you deeply love and trust, positively impact your community, enjoy the flexibility that private ownership offers, and feel passionately proud of the family brand, history, and nostalgia. That's just part of the great things about family business. Now back to the hard parts.

When Responsibility Becomes a Strength Overused

In the 1995 film *Tommy Boy*, Chris Farley plays Tommy, the incompetent and immature son of an auto parts entrepreneur. Classically entitled, Tommy enjoys the privileges of family business ownership without taking on any of the corresponding responsibility. When his father dies, Tommy slowly steps up, takes responsibility, and eventually saves the family business.

Although this entitled heir stereotype exists for a reason, most of the leaders I work with feel more responsibility than privilege.[43] When it's your name on the door, your family's reputation in the community, your legacy to steward for the next generation, the burden can feel weighty.

Thomas from chapter 2 described it like this. "Our name is on the buildings and on the trucks driving around the region. At funerals, a lot of people say to me, 'My uncle worked for you.' That carries responsibility in our family's eyes," he said.

Most of the family employees I've met work hard, if not harder than their nonfamily coworkers. They often feel held to higher standards than their nonfamily peers. Eager to avoid the "entitled" label associated with an overuse of privilege, many work longer hours for less pay. This overfocus on responsibilities converts what looks like nepotism from the outside into performance pressure on the inside.

This theme of intense, self-imposed pressure arose often in my interviews for this book, as you'll see in the stories of Saleem, Quinn, Joseph, and Robin. When Saleem, a thirty-six-year-old G2 CEO, suddenly lost his father fifteen years earlier, he worked day and night to recover the family's reputation in his community in India. The business was deeply challenged at the time. Employees had not been

---

43 That may be due to selection bias. Those who favor privilege may be less inclined to seek the support of coaches.

paid in five months, the business carried considerable debt, and his cousins were collecting a salary without doing any work.

Saleem almost lost the business and their family home. "I felt so much pressure to maintain the integrity of the family name, which has been around for thirty years. All the dealings with suppliers, employees, and customers are governed by that name," he said. Failure was not an option; his family's reputation was too important to risk, and he felt responsible for saving it.

Similarly, G2 CEO Quinn was desperate to turn around his family business for his twenty-eight-year-old son. "As much as I would like to quit working, I feel this obligation to my son," Quinn said. "I don't want to walk out one day and have him struggle or fail. I want him to take over a less stressful situation. Nobody should live under this stress. It's never-ending. Not healthy."

Joseph (G2 CEO from chapter 4) sees family business leadership as "a no-win situation when you are a G2 or G3 leader. If you succeed, it's because your father gave it to you. If you fail, your father gave you this business, and you ran it into the ground." Joseph was sensitive to the judgment of family and nonfamily alike. "Employees are always looking at family members and asking, 'Are you doing your fair share of work?'"

On top of the self-pressure, Joseph felt direct pressure from his father. "Dad rode me really hard. One day, one of our employees pulled me aside and said, 'Your dad loves you; he just has a hard time showing it.' The pressure I felt was *huge*," Joseph said.

Many leaders I interviewed felt generational pressure to keep the dream alive. While stewarding his great-grandfather's business, Robin, a sixty-four-year-old G4 CEO, felt responsible for carrying on the legacy, despite his only son's weak prospects at leadership. Robin wondered if it was time to sell, then recalled that his great-grandfather started this business 150 years ago the next month. "How can *I* be the one that brings this legacy to an end?" Robin said. "I've kicked this can down the road for five years so far. What's another five?"

In their 2014 book *The Voice of the Rising Generation*, James Hughes,

Susan Massenzio, and Keith Whitaker describe a common phenomenon that afflicts descendants of highly successful entrepreneurs.[44] Upon the death of such a founder, a metaphorical black hole can emerge, sucking in the dreams and aspirations of future generations who feel obligated to carry forth the founder's dream. This black hole—this pressure to perpetuate an ancestor's dream—burdens the descendants who may otherwise choose to chart their own course but feel pressure to steward for *their* descendants, just like their parents did for them.

Jim (age fifty-two, G2 CEO) devoted his entire career to living out his father's dream, and he now resents the time he spent leading his family business. "I spent my adult life trying to live my own legacy and ended up spending thirty years carrying out my father's."

To combat this tendency, Hughes, Massenzio, and Whitaker advise descendants to pursue their own dreams—find their own voice. Although this process doesn't preclude descendants from carrying forward the family business, it helps rising-generation leaders make the choice *consciously*, not by default or due to internal or external pressure. Ensuring the rising generation has agency over their lives lessens the likelihood that they will confuse their ancestor's dream for their own.

Still, even when leaders know what they are signing up for, it can be hard to turn away. Trent (age forty-six, G4 CEO) witnessed three generations of misery before choosing to take it on himself. "None of us thought Dad liked what he did," recalls Trent. "And he didn't! It's a hard business with low profits." Trent found no pleasure in working with family. "The previous generation was so toxic, and I almost *hated* my father. Hated the sight of him. We were together day-to-day, and I hated seeing him over the holidays."

Trent went on to describe the "huge physical consequences of stress." His great-grandfather was an alcoholic at fifty. His grandfather

---

44   James E. Hughes, Jr., Susan E. Massenzio and Keith Whitaker, *The Voice of the Rising Generation: Family Wealth and Wisdom*, (Hoboken: John Wiley & Sons, Inc., 2014).

got sick at fifty. His father was severely depressed at fifty. "It seems to hit our family in our early fifties," he observed.

Although Trent is seeking ways to disrupt this ancestral pattern, he continues to lead the business and is planning for his son to succeed him as the fifth generation leader. "I'm encouraging most of my kids to find their own wings, but my third grader wants to be a boss."

When Privilege Becomes a Strength Overused

Although I encounter leaders suffering from overperformance more than underperformance, family member underperformance isn't uncommon. Some family members collect salaries yet do no work at all—clear evidence of the power of the family mindset.

After cofounding a business with his brother and his wife, Yaniva watched his sister-in-law work less and less while she charged personal expenses through the business more and more. After years of stifling his frustrations, he finally addressed his concerns, and they all agreed to change their compensation to a commission-based model: you get paid when you produce.

Sadly, within a year, Yaniva discovered that his brother and sister-in-law had fixed their high salaries, and Yaniva was the only one on commission. Infuriated, he quit.

"Leaving the family business was one of the most difficult decisions I have ever made," said Yaniva. He was terrified of leaving what he knew to forge a new future for his family. "The sleepless nights, the stress, the uncertainty of not knowing what's next and what and how I would reestablish myself, while still having the responsibility of raising a family . . ." Nevertheless, "leaving was one of my best decisions," he reflected confidently.

PRO TIP

In any polarity, when someone leans hard on one pole, they are certain to experience its overuses. To mitigate this, find ways to engage the other end of the pole. This is especially useful in the privileges :: responsibility polarity.

Using a reference from *The Simpsons*,[45] if Bart Simpson is overfocused on privileges, give him the corresponding responsibility he has earned; then hold him accountable. Similarly, if Lisa Simpson is overfocused on responsibility, encourage her to enjoy some of the privileges she has earned so she doesn't burn out or overperform for others.

BOTTOM LINE: EXPAND YOUR EFFECTIVENESS BY SPRINKLING YOUR LESS-PREFERRED POLE INTO YOUR LEADERSHIP STYLE. IF YOU ARE HUMBLE, EXPERIMENT WITH BOLDNESS, AND VICE VERSA.

Entitlement Isn't Always an Overuse of Privilege

Despite its reputation, the overuse of privileges may have little to do with entitlement or skill gaps. Other dynamics were at play with G2 brothers Peter and Maks. Both in their midthirties, they led different departments in their mother's business, but Peter's underperformance almost blew the whole business up.

It looked like entitlement on the surface. Peter interrupted his golf game enough to show up at the office about ten hours a week, and he was standoffish and unapproachable while there. His younger brother Maks worked a full workweek but, leaning on the family mindset, didn't believe it was his place to challenge his brother's behavior. Maks's wife, Lenore, however, had no problem with conflict. She also worked in the business and had plenty to say about Peter's underperformance. Interestingly, the more she spoke up, the more Peter checked out.

It turns out that Peter hated working with his sister-in-law. "When Maks and I joined Mom's business, I was excited to work with him. My brother is my best friend." But Peter hated the marital dynamics

---

45 *The Simpsons* is a famous cartoon series in the US. "The Simpsons," Wikipedia, accessed March 2, 2024, https://en.wikipedia.org/wiki/The_Simpsons.

he saw between Maks and Lenore. "I hate how Lenore bullies Maks, and I hate that he doesn't stand up for himself," Peter complained. "I signed up for working with my brother. I did *not* sign up for working with a two-headed monster."

With some support, Peter found a productive way to express his concerns to Maks, and after several heart-to-hearts, some of which included Lenore, Peter reengaged with the business at one-hundred-percent effort. (A year later, Maks and Lenore divorced.)

In a different example, sometimes behavior that appears entitled is, in fact, a mental health struggle. When I interviewed Saleem for this book, he described his leadership style as "not overly ambitious. I can get by on three to four hours of work per day. This business has become a lifestyle for me." He continued, "I had no boss when I took over the business at age twenty-one after my father died. At first, I worked constantly, but once the company turned around, I took a lot of holidays, didn't invest in the business, bought a sports car, new house." It was tempting to assume he leaned more into the privileges than the responsibilities of leadership.

However, three days after the interview, Saleem emailed me to express how grateful he was to reflect on his role as leader of his family's business. The interview spurred some self-reflection and gave him a higher-level perspective, a perspective he hadn't considered in the past. In one email, he wrote, "As I mentioned earlier, the *one* recurring theme in my life has been my daily struggle with motivation. Even today. The reason that I am replying to this email on Tuesday evening is that I have entirely skipped work today, stayed in bed, and watched movies the entire day."

That made me pause. I had read that staying in bed day after day can be a sign of depression. I took a risk and told him about the connection between depression and staying in bed all day. Had he considered counseling? He hadn't, but suddenly, the dots started to connect in his head.

A year later, he emailed me with effervescent gratitude for having the courage to suggest therapy. As it turns out, Saleem hadn't yet grieved for the loss of his father. After processing his grief with a therapist, he is transformed. Not only is he enthusiastically engaged in his work, but he has also started a new business. He wasn't entitled a year ago—he was depressed.

It's The Identity, Stupid

Much like a big ego sometimes overcompensates for low self-esteem, entitled behavior can be a mask for low self-worth. Growing up in a successful family business, surrounded by outsized talent, or in the shadow of an icon can be hard. You can't help but compare yourself to others and ask, *Am I as good as they are? What do I have to offer? Where can I add value?*

Without comfortable answers to these questions, it can be hard to form an identity that makes you feel proud of who you are. Forming an identity around your strengths is a normal phase of adult maturation. According to American Psychologist Dr. Abraham Maslow, it's one of our basic human needs.[46] It's how you feel good about yourself and how you want to be seen in society. When your skills don't measure up to a standard set in your mind, it's tempting to seek other ways to fit into society, such as affiliating with your successful family.

That's when an overuse of privilege can result in entitled behavior. Maybe it's an Instagram post with you and your friends opening a bottle of champagne on your private jet. Maybe it's in the fashion and bling you wear to fit into the glamorous social scene. Maybe it's the low handicap you maintain on the golf course. Whatever the behavior, it's designed to signal that you are special—that you deserve to fit in.

Underperformance and Overperformance

Underperformance by some family members (privilege) is often paired with overperformance by other family members (responsibility),

---

[46] "Maslow's hierarchy of needs," Wikipedia, accessed March 2, 2024, https://en.wikipedia.org/wiki/Maslow%27s_hierarchy_of_needs.

and once this pattern is established, it's difficult to upend because it's self-reinforcing.

Benjamin, a fifty-seven-year-old G3 CEO, put enormous pressure on himself to outwork his underperforming father and uncles. "In G2, some family members had positions because of their last name, not because they were good managers or leaders. That doesn't perpetuate longevity, growth, or succession." So Benjamin balanced the ledger. "As a family leader, you gotta be the best," he said. "You're going to work the hardest, longest, be the smartest if you can. When everyone else is going home, you stay."

Benjamin isn't an anomaly. Many family business leaders devote themselves to their family business to avoid the "entitled" label that comes with unearned privilege. However, that devotion results in taking on more responsibility than appropriate.

Once forty-five-year-old entrepreneur Isaac achieved business success, his family leaned on him for (what felt like) everything. "They expected me to be the proxy patriarch. If I can run a business, then I can manage their money." Even his father relied on Isaac by granting him full powers over the estate. "All the money, estate planning, asset management, medical powers of attorney, executors of the estate . . . it all went to me based on my success of running a business." Eventually, Isaac stumbled into conflicts of interest and stopped overperforming for the entire family. "I won't do that as a father, brother, or cousin. Not anymore," he said. Now his siblings share some of the responsibility, and the family is better off for it.

The fallout from an underperformance/overperformance dynamic can be fatal to a family business. Both G3 brothers, Spencer and Travis, agreed that Travis was the slacker. One day, Travis taunted Spencer. "You're going to run the company someday, and I'll get half the pay!"

Over my dead body, you will, thought Spencer. When a consolidator offered to buy the business a few years later, Travis's taunting played in the back of Spencer's mind. "It wasn't the only reason to sell," he said, "but I didn't want the family business to break up the family.

This business had been my life. I earned it the hard way, but I was very worried about my brother's entitled mindset." Spencer sold the family business.

The pairing of overperformance and underperformance can become a vicious cycle. The more one family member overperforms, the more another underperforms, and interestingly, resentment can smolder on both sides. Not only did this phenomenon lead to the sale of Jim's family business, but it also destroyed the relationship between Jim and his brother, Domino.

It started out well. Jim led sales while Domino led sourcing, both reporting to Dad. Domino suddenly became CEO when their father died suddenly but "CEO in title only," according to Jim. "Domino didn't really step up as a leader, so, slowly, I stepped into the role. Nothing was ever said. I just picked up the balls," said Jim.

Eventually, they became copresidents in title, earning the same salary, but Domino stayed focused on sourcing, and Jim picked up everything else. "If I see a problem, I fix it," Jim said. "As I kept taking on more responsibilities, I became the leader organically. We never actually discussed it."

Jim continued, "I became extremely resentful because I was working really hard, and Domino wouldn't follow through with anything. He complained that no matter what he did, I would criticize him." Feeling inadequate and picked on, Domino checked out. The more Domino withdrew, the more Jim stepped in, and this cycle continued until Jim was running the entire business.

"We were both very angry and very hurt," Jim said. Eventually, the business began to decline. They hired a turn-around consultant who recommended that Domino take a 30 percent cut in pay, given his limited contribution to the business. Reluctantly, Domino agreed to the pay cut, but the business continued to decline until it could no longer afford Domino's salary at all. "Our business was not performing, and one of us had to go," Jim said. "It couldn't be me because I *was* the business!"

Although terrified by his employment prospects as an unemployed fifty-five-year-old, Domino left the business and blamed Jim for it. Within two years, Jim sold the business at a fraction of its peak value, and the brothers haven't spoken since. "I don't know if we'll ever have a relationship again," Jim said. "It's a struggle to balance the role as a sibling with the role as the leader. The two aren't often in the same place. There's guilt. You can't serve them both. Something is going to suffer no matter what. I tried pleasing everyone for eighteen years. It didn't work," said Jim.

Jim's painful story highlights the anguish that the business mindset and family mindset polarity can evoke. Leading with the business mindset, Jim tried to salvage the business. Leading with the family mindset, Domino never forgave Jim for squeezing him out. Jim felt damned if you do and damned if you don't—a no-win situation. Fortunately, there is a third way, which we will introduce in chapters 9 and 10.

In the next chapter, let's explore how the family :: business polarity, when framed as a problem, leads to conflict.

Questions for Chapter 5

1. Which pole do you lean toward: privileges or responsibilities?
2. If you overfocus on responsibilities, how do you manage the pressure you feel stewarding your family business? What strategies can you experiment with to mitigate that stress?
3. If you tend to overperform relative to others, what impact does it have on their performance?
4. Conversely, if you overemphasize privileges (and be honest with yourself here), what fear or unmet need is driving this lopsided behavior? How can you take on some responsibility commensurate with your privilege to mitigate entitlement?
5. If you tend to underperform relative to others, what impact does it have on their performance?

"Whether it's in the office or around the family dinner table, don't avoid honest, clear conflict. It will get you the best car price, the higher salary, and the largest donation. It will also save your marriage, your friendship, and your family. One can only be an exceptional negotiator, and a great person, by both listening and speaking clearly and empathetically; by treating counterpart—and oneself—with dignity and respect; and most of all by being honest about what one wants and what one can—and cannot—do. Every negotiation, every conversation, every moment of life, is a series of small conflicts that, managed well, can rise to creative beauty. Embrace them."

—Chris Voss, Author of
Never Split the Difference.

CHAPTER 6
FOSTERING CONSTRUCTIVE CONFLICT

"*If he ignores me one more time, I'm going to tank both of our businesses,*" said Tricia. "*He hasn't answered any of my emails in a week! I just need simple answers to my questions, but he disrespects me every time I try to talk to him. I've had it!*" *Tricia is prepared to destroy her cousin's business, even if it means destroying her own to do it.*

Second cousins Tricia (sixty-four) and Harry (forty-six) don't share a childhood despite their shared great-grandparents. What they do share is fifty-fifty ownership of two different businesses headquartered in the same office. Tricia is the CEO of Tortoise Electronics, a stable cash cow that is slowly being disrupted by newer technologies, and Harry is the CEO of Hare Designs, a fast-growing e-tailer that is sweeping the nation. For convenience, they share administrative functions such as HR, legal, and office management.

With a gift for details and process, Tricia is well suited for her role as CEO of thin-margined Tortoise Electronics. She wants to enjoy her last two years as CEO and glide into retirement.

Harry, in contrast, joined the family business after a stint in management consulting to grow their new startup into a national e-tailing business. His gift for big-picture strategy, online sales, and infrastructure investment serves the needs of his rapidly growing e-tailing business well.

But Harry never wants to set eyes on Tricia again. "Her petty obsession with minutia drives me crazy. I don't care what color the cafeteria plates should be. She can pick any color she wants," said Harry. "Her ridiculous questions drag my attention away from my priorities. I've tried to be nice about it, but I'm through. I have to ignore her completely so that I can focus on the things that matter."

◆ ◆ ◆

Although few family businesses experience this level of sustained conflict, all family businesses experience conflict, whether overt or covert. Conflict is unavoidable. In fact, conflict is *necessary* in a family business. It's the *type* of conflict that determines whether it's constructive or destructive. Constructive conflict builds relationships and leads to better outcomes. Destructive conflict consumes emotional energy and undermines connection.

Families with good conflict management skills *have a competitive advantage*. As Di Loreto and Isaacson wrote, "Fake harmony can be far more damaging than fireworks, because it causes families to avoid making difficult, but important, decisions about the business or the family."[47] They go on to describe the risk of fake harmony: "a 'cliff event'—an unaddressed conflict that builds and builds over time until it erupts into far more serious and complex arguments."

Take sisters Caroline and Belle from chapter 4. Their "cliff event" seemed so small. When Caroline took Belle's teenage daughters shopping, they bought skinny jeans, and when Belle found out, she erupted with anger, convinced that Caroline was intentionally

---

47 Nick Di Loreto and Alison Isaacson, "Avoiding Conflict Will Only Hurt Your Family Business," *Harvard Business Review*, October 5, 2022, https://hbr.org/2022/10/avoiding-conflict-will-only-hurt-your-family-business

purchasing age-inappropriate clothes for her daughters. Caroline intended generosity—buying gifts was how she expressed her love—but after decades of low trust and high conflict, Belle believed Caroline had malicious intent. That cliff event took place over ten years ago, and the sisters haven't spoken since.

By comparison, Mason, from chapter 4, believes that his family's investment in communication is the primary fuel for their company's success. He said, "The biggest lesson I've learned is that communication is key. It's not easy. That phase when we had weekly meetings for years—that's the one thing I pin our success on. Learning to communicate is huge."

Avoid Conflict :: Seek Conflict

Harry and Tricia from the opening story are stuck in a pernicious fight-flight loop. One avoids conflict, and the other seeks it. When Tricia asks Harry a question, Harry avoids conflict by ignoring her (flight). That makes Tricia feel disrespected and angry, so she seeks conflict by asserting herself with Harry (fight). Harry then avoids Tricia again (flight), provoking Tricia to demand Harry's attention more forcefully (fight), thus prompting Harry to withdraw further, etc. Because this destructive cycle has never been disrupted, both cousins' behavior has become extreme.

The opposing mindsets in a family business make it hard. Although the business mindset can tolerate conflict, the family mindset craves harmony. Our family is *supposed to be* our safe place; it's where we are supposed to feel a deep and unconditional sense of love and belonging. Therefore, when we fight with family, that sense of belonging is at risk and triggers the reactive fight/flight/freeze/fawn response. This chapter is intended to help you learn how to engage in constructive conflict so you don't experience the overuses of avoiding conflict (artificial harmony) or seeking conflict (mean-spirited personal attacks).[48]

---

48 Pat Lencioni, The *Five Dysfunctions of a Team,* (Hoboken: Wiley, 2002).

Disharmony feels icky. Literally. Close your eyes and imagine you are about to engage in conflict. How does your body respond physiologically? For me, my heart rate increases, and my heartbeat thumps harder. I get fidgety, and I want that physical discomfort to go away. It's much easier for me to avoid the conflict than to tolerate the discomfort of conflict.

PRO TIP

If my sister calls out my selfish behavior, and I feel hurt, *I'm making myself feel hurt.* Maybe I fear there's some truth to her assessment. Maybe I fear someone else will see me that same way. Bottom line, I don't want the assessment to be true, so I defend my ego and react.

This hurt comes from a disconnect between expectations and reality. My expectation is that I'm not selfish. The reality is that my sister sees me as selfish. Similarly, my expectation may be that I'm ready to lead the business. The reality may be that my aunt doesn't agree. When that disconnect between expectations and reality is the source of the pain, *replace the hurt with curiosity*. What makes my sister see me as selfish? What makes my aunt believe I'm not ready to take over leadership? Leaning in with curiosity can ease the pain by closing that gap between expectations and reality, thus minimizing the reactive behavior that comes from defending your ego.

If my reactive nature is to control (fight), I might accuse her of being even more selfish. If my reactive nature is to withdraw (flee), I might hang up the phone or stomp out of the room. If my reactive nature is to freeze, I might be silent and hope she stops talking. Last, if my reactive nature is to appease (fawn), I might own up to these negative assessments, whether I believe they are true or not.

The truth is, I'm a recovering fawner, and I tend to take responsibility for things, whether or not I'm even involved. Conversely, my sister tends to blame outward. So, when something goes awry, there's one thing she and I agree on: it's my fault. Oof!

Over time, I've learned not to overreact to other people's negative assessments of me. Some of them are true, which is helpful data. I let in the assessments I can learn from and let the rest roll off my back. Some of them are not true, yet it's helpful to know how others perceive me. I've stopped defending myself against other people's assessments of me. They are simply another opinion, and so what if someone has a different opinion about me than I do about myself? Both opinions can coexist. No big whoop. Now, I'm just grateful when someone has the courage to share one.

BOTTOM LINE: DON'T SHY AWAY FROM CONFLICT FOR FEAR OF BEING WRONG. CONVERT YOUR TYPICAL FIGHT/FLIGHT/FREEZE/FAWN RESPONSE TO SIMPLE CURIOSITY.

Lack of Conflict Doesn't Guarantee Agreement

Research shows that the alternative to conflict isn't agreement; it's apathy and disengagement. "Teams unable to foster substantive conflict ultimately achieve, on average, lower performance."[49] So when we avoid conflict, we miss opportunities to challenge assumptions, question beliefs, see the bigger system, explore alternatives, and collaborate to reach a better outcome. Avoiding conflict doesn't make conflict go away. It just simmers below the surface until a cliff event unleashes the pent-up energy.

Not all cliff events lead to disaster. Often, the rupture from a cliff event precipitates meaningful change—change that needed to happen but wouldn't have happened without the cliff event. When cliff events take place, attend to the rupture and look for what needs to change to improve the situation.

Although many of us avoid conflict so we don't hurt other family

---

49 Kathleen M. Eisenhardt, Jean L. Kahwajy, and L.J. Bourgeois III, "How Management Teams Can Have a Good Fight," *Harvard Business Review*, July-August 1997.

members, there's an important distinction between hurt and harm.[50] Hurt is a temporary pain that may help us grow. Harm is a pain that inflicts long-term damage. Sometimes it's kinder to inflict a little hurt to avert greater harm.

For example, recall Aaron from chapter 3, whose father chose Aaron over his son-in-law Frank to succeed him as CEO. Desperate to avoid the discomfort of conflict, Aaron's father never discussed it with Frank, and Frank was devastated. Not only was he passed over, but nobody even spoke about it with him. This lack of upfront communication became a breaking point in the family, leading to a permanent rift and straining Aaron's relationship with Frank as well as Aaron's sister, Frank's wife.

Aaron's wife described it well. "Aaron's dad was a big pleaser. He didn't have the communication skills to deal with Frank. It was too hard for him to say the hard things. That was the beginning of the end." Avoiding short-term hurt leads to long-term harm, so to avert harm, sometimes we must inflict some hurt.

PRO TIP

Kind isn't always nice, and nice isn't always kind. Nice is telling someone they look great even though they have spinach in their teeth. Kind is telling them about the spinach, even if it makes you uncomfortable to say it. Be kind.

In her book *Radical Candor*,[51] Kim Scott shares a helpful framework for giving feedback. She describes radical candor as the combination of both challenging directly and caring personally. When I'm giving tough feedback, I hold tons of love in my heart and ensure that I'm addressing their behavior, not their identity. There is an enormous difference between pointing out bad

---

50 Melissa Mitchell-Blitch, *In the Company of Family: How to Thrive When Business is Personal*, (Charleston: Eredita Consulting LLC, 2020).
51 Kim Scott, *Radical Candor: Be a Kick-Ass Boss without Losing Your Humanity*, (New York: St. Martin's Publishing Group, 2019).

behavior and telling someone they are a bad *person*.

BOTTOM LINE: DON'T SHY AWAY FROM CONFLICT BECAUSE YOU WANT TO BE NICE. INSTEAD, BE KIND BY RESPECTFULLY SHARING YOUR ASSESSMENTS SO OTHERS CAN LEARN. IF THEY DISAGREE OR TAKE IT POORLY, THAT IS THEIR CHOICE.

It's Hard to Know Your Culture When Your Culture Is All You Know

Ethan (age sixty-two, former CEO) didn't recognize how conflict-avoidant his family business culture was until after he sold it. "One of our biggest problems was false agreement within our family," he said, describing false agreement as when two people pretend that they agree on a decision when, in truth, they don't. Instead, they go along to get along. "Compulsive false agreement is one reason my brother left the business."

Ethan regrets that his nonfamily leaders failed to share developmental feedback with family employees because family members didn't mature as leaders. "Our nonfamily leaders in high positions gave family members too much of a pass," Ethan said. "If I were to do something over again, I'd address that. Performance management wasn't perfect because it takes a pretty tough individual to be able to tune out the fact that it's a family member."

Family members carried inherent power in the eyes of his nonfamily leaders, making feedback risky. That's why fostering a culture that values developmental feedback for all employees—including family—helps an entire company mature, especially in an environment where it's hard to speak truth to power for fear of backlash.

Performance Reviews? Bah!

Few of the family business leaders I interviewed provided ongoing leadership development or even conducted performance reviews for family members—less than 5 percent! During the twenty years I spent in large corporate environments before leading my father's business, I regularly received developmental feedback and leadership training. In fact, as I progressed into larger leadership roles, I was offered even *more* professional training and development. The more I advanced, the more development I received.

Not so with the family business leaders I interviewed. Most described feedback as either sugarcoated, overly harsh, or, most often, nonexistent. As Trent from chapter 5 described, "My father didn't address performance issues. He had no development plan for himself or his kids."

This aversion to leadership development is a competitive *dis*advantage for family businesses. Few are willing to tolerate the discomfort of developmental feedback, even when such leadership development serves the business mindset of growing profits. Sure, performance feedback can feel uncomfortable, but developmental feedback is critical to enhancing leadership effectiveness. (Read on to learn how.)

In reflecting on his tenure as G2 CEO, Quinn, from chapter 5, acknowledged that his ego prevented him from seeking ways to improve. "I didn't go someplace to develop leadership skills. I was offered an opportunity to join a peer group, but I couldn't do it. I probably declined because I was concerned about exposing my failings," he admitted. "I felt threatened, so I created a situation where I wouldn't be threatened. The business has suffered as a result."

He goes on to describe a cultural aversion to feedback that spans generations. "My father never addresses anything with me, and I don't do it with my employees either. I regret it. There's more drama in the business than we should have as a result," Quinn said. "We have no review process at all. I was never reviewed. If I did something my father disapproved of, he just got angry. With my son, I have a wariness about giving him feedback because of how he deals with criticism."

The justifications were endless. Lucas, a G2 CEO, admits he's avoiding family disharmony. "Poor performance is not dealt with as straight on as it should be. We go around the person to get the result we need," he said. "It takes a long time, and sometimes we don't get what we want. I tend to avoid confrontation with my brother. It's easier not to address it. It keeps family harmony."

G2 CEO Yannick finds it especially hard with siblings. "Giving honest feedback to an employee is hard enough. Giving it to a sibling is almost impossible. You can't properly manage a sibling—there's too much baggage from the sibling relationship," he says.

What a missed opportunity in family businesses. Yes, growth is unpleasant, but *there is no comfort in the growth zone and no growth in the comfort zone.* As Melissa Mitchell-Blitch writes in *In the Company of Family: How to Thrive When Business Is Personal*,[52] "If we want to help others enhance their skills, we can do so through honest feedback. Critique need not be critical; it can be constructive. Constructive criticism may temporarily hurt, but it will not cause lasting harm. Like strength training, through which muscles grow by being challenged, the temporary pain of constructive criticism can lead to long-term growth." I highly recommend this book for those who want to build their skills in drawing healthy boundaries.

In a noted exception, Daniel (G3 retired chairperson) took delight in creating a culture of feedback. "When I was president, I evaluated my brother on a yearly basis, no different from any other employee. No special pass for family, nor do they want any special passes. They want to be judged on merit only," he said. His culture valued meritocracy, a norm of the business mindset. "Some members of G4 work really hard and some not as hard. Those who work hard assume more responsibility and get big pay increases. Those who don't . . . don't."

PRO TIP

When you are on the *receiving* end of critical feedback, you are responsible for drawing appropriate boundaries. Assess what part of the feedback is helpful and what is not. As Mitchell-Blitch

---

52   Melissa Mitchell-Blitch, *In the Company of Family: How to Thrive When Business is Personal*, (Charleston: Eredita Consulting LLC, 2020), 73.

writes, the purpose of boundaries is "to let in the good and keep out the bad." If the feedback isn't accurate or helpful, don't let it in. If there is something to learn from it, let it in and learn. If you aren't sure, sit with it and explore what is uncomfortable about sowing the seeds of wisdom.

Reaction to conflict tends to show up in four ways: fight (confront the conflict; challenge), flight (withdraw from conflict; protect), freeze (do nothing), and fawn (appease; comply). To grow more tolerant of interpersonal disharmony, notice your body's reaction to conflict, and get curious. Can you observe and tolerate your body's reaction? It's just a sensation that came alive because your amygdala was hijacked. Ask yourself what feels risky, and notice if your body's reaction is proportional to the risk. If it's disproportionately high, practice the self-management techniques described in chapter 2. If it's an extreme overreaction, find a good therapist—there may be something else going on.

As you improve your emotional intelligence, you build greater tolerance for the discomfort of conflict so you can stay clearheaded and calm in the face of other people's reactive behavior. This will help you make fact-based decisions instead of reacting to relational dynamics.

BOTTOM LINE: LEARN TO EMBRACE FEEDBACK AS A GIFT, NOT AS A FAILURE.

I'm Not Saying It's Easy

It takes genuine maturity to hear feedback from family members without getting defensive. Although a "captain of industry" in his broader community, Isaac (from chapter 5) and his siblings sometimes regress to childhood communication patterns at work. "My fifty-three-year-old sister will ask, 'What will Dad say about that?' and I have to stop myself from panicking like I did as a child. What is Dad going to do, spank me?" Isaac chuckled. "He's ninety years old!"

Isaac has learned to address conflict right away. "I don't let things linger," he said. "I'm all about direct communication. Anytime I feel family members step on my toes, I'm right on it, face-to-face. We do it professionally, productively, and at the same time, we are all eight years old, and sometimes we scream at each other." He chuckled.

Task Conflict and Relationship Conflict

Conflict can be separated into two types: task conflict and relationship conflict. Task conflict is people versus problem (should the logo be green or yellow?), whereas relationship conflict is person versus person (does she think I'm stupid?). Research by Adam Grant shows that task conflict is *desirable*[53]; relationship conflict is not.

Task conflict is important because it helps us see the bigger picture and understand our challenges better. It uncovers other people's strengths and shakes up entrenched beliefs that no longer work. Because task conflict isn't personal, it can be spirited but intellectual.

Bottom line: task conflict yields better outcomes.

In contrast, relationship conflict yields worse outcomes. We burn our energy defending our egos and proving to others that they are wrong instead of partnering to seek a better way. According to Adam Grant's research, relationship conflict is more destructive than productive. "When a clash gets personal and emotional, we become self-righteous preachers of our own views, spiteful prosecutors of the other side, or single-minded politicians who dismiss opinions that don't come from our side," he writes in *Think Again*. This kind of conflict pushes people apart, impeding access to the benefits of task conflict.

The sweet spot for constructive conflict in a family business is embracing task conflict and mitigating relationship conflict. However, that's a tall ask for those of us who have an aversion to any kind of conflict whatsoever or mistake challenges to our ideas as threats to our ego. Fortunately, there is a remedy: trust. Trust helps ensure that hearty task conflict doesn't devolve into debilitating relationship conflict.

---

53   Adam Grant, *Think Again* (New York: Viking, 2021)

PRO TIP

Knowing your innate conflict style can prepare you for healthy conflict. Much research has been conducted on conflict styles. Stemming from work initiated by Black and Mouton in the 1960s, Kenneth Thomas and Ralph Kilmann crafted an assessment (TKI[54]) that depicts five different predispositions or styles that people bring to conflict. Each style has advantages and disadvantages, and no single style is ideal for all situations. However, one style reigns supreme in maintaining long-term, healthy relationships. Identifying your preferred style may help you improve your conflict skills.

BOTTOM LINE: BUILDING CAPACITY TO ENGAGE IN CONFLICT APPROPRIATELY, USING EACH OF THE FIVE TYPES OF CONFLICT, BROADENS YOUR LEADERSHIP TOOL KIT AND RESPONSE-AGILITY.

The Importance of Trust

In high-trust family business cultures, conflict doesn't feel uncomfortable or scary. It's okay to be wrong. Family leaders in high-trust cultures aren't sidetracked by emotional distractions; they ask direct questions and address issues openly because nobody's ego is on the line. With trusting relationships, families can robustly debate ideas with the confidence to disagree without fear of repercussions. They can hold each other and themselves accountable to their commitments. They feel safe enough to give and receive feedback. In fact, trust is considered a unique competitive advantage[55] for family businesses.

So why is trust low in some families? Maybe it's because our earliest

---

54 "Thomas-Kilmann Instrument (TKI)," Kilmann Diagnostics, accessed March 2, 2024, https://kilmanndiagnostics.com/assessments/thomas-kilmann-instrument-one-assessment-person/

55 Mohammad Azizi, Masood Salmani Bidgoli, and Ameneh Seddighian Bidgoli, "Trust in family businesses: A more comprehensive empirical review," *Taylor & Francis Online*, accessed March 2, 2024, https://www.tandfonline.com/doi/full/10.1080/23311975.2017.1359445.

sibling interactions take place when we are immature. During adolescence, we are self-interested monsters. We are not trustworthy—we are wired to be selfish. This is a normal stage of development (most) everyone passes through,[56] yet that's when our earliest sibling memories are formed.

When we enter high school, our focus shifts outward, and we care more about the opinions of our friends[57] than those of our family. Eventually, we launch into the world and continue to mature, yet with those immature sibling memories planted deep in our psyches, we regress to eight-year-olds during family gatherings. We may be high-functioning adults in the big world, but at Thanksgiving dinner, we revert to adolescent hierarchies and behaviors. This phenomenon has a name: holiday regression.[58]

My four siblings and I experienced this ourselves. In our forties, we realized that we were remarkably unkind to each other. We treated our friends much better than we treated each other, so we decided to change our sibling dynamic by gathering for what we called G5 Summits.[59] At our first summit, we spent ninety minutes arguing like eight-year-olds about communication protocols. Fortunately, we kept at it once a month for a few years, and we now have (mostly) mature, adult relationships with each other.

Family members in low-trust family businesses experience holiday regression all year long, which is why it's so important to cultivate trust and develop leaders. When we are stuck in childhood patterns, taking things personally and protecting ourselves from hurt, we're not focused on the business. We're focused on our egos.

---

56   Saul Mcleod, "Piaget's Theory And Stages Of Cognitive Development," *Simply Psychology*, Updated on January 24, 2024, https://www.simplypsychology.org/piaget.html.
57   Natali Mallel (Morad), "Part 1: How To Be An Adult— Kegan's Theory of Adult Development," *Medium*, September 28, 2017, https://medium.com/@NataliMorad/how-to-be-an-adult-kegans-theory-of-adult-development-d63f4311b553.
58   Rachel Myrow, "When a Visit Home Triggers 'Holiday Regression,'" *KQED*, December 23, 2019, https://www.kqed.org/forum/2010101875033/when-a-visit-home-triggers-holiday-regression.
59   We were five siblings, hence the "Group of five" or "G5." To be clear, we are third generation, not fifth generation.

Alas, trust is destroyed in a flash and takes time to rebuild. It regrows from fairness, honesty, forgiveness, reliability, vulnerability, forthright communication, and *both* repeated positive interactions *and* through brave conversations. Why brave conversations? Conflict inevitably arises in all close relationships, and brave conversations are a path through conflict. More on brave conversations later. First, let's understand how to address task conflict.

Embracing Task Conflict

Task conflict is a people versus problem conflict. When leaders simply disagree about how to solve a problem, they can partner with each other to explore solutions together. These leaders are metaphorically on the same side of the table, and the "problem" is on the other side.

A simple process to work through task conflict follows some of the best practices from negotiations.[60] Follow this ALIGN process to reach agreement.

Agree
Learn
Invest
Generate
Nothing

Agree on the goal. Make sure everyone clearly understands the problem you are trying to solve. As Einstein famously said, "If I had an hour to solve a problem, I'd spend fifty-five minutes thinking about the problem and five minutes thinking about solutions." Framing the problem well sets the stage for how the solution will be found. At a minimum, define your shared interests in working through the problem.

---

60 This approach borrows from Roger Fisher and William Ury, *Getting to Yes*, (Boston: Houghton Mifflin, 1981). For emotional negotiations, I recommend Chris Voss *Never Split the Difference: Negotiating As If Your Life Depended On It*, (New York: Harper Business, 2016).

Learn the other people's interests. What do the others want? Focus on their interests (e.g., a 20 percent net margin), not their position (e.g., we should sunset this product). Be sure to share *your* interests, not your position. Ask, "For the sake of what do you take that position?" to shift from a position to an interest.

Invest in their outcome. Help others reach their goals. When you help other people achieve their interests, they are more willing to help you achieve yours. If investing in others' outcomes comes at a meaningful sacrifice for you, communicate your boundaries.

Generate ideas. Let creativity fly. Brainstorm a variety of strategies to reach your goal. Release the attachment to the first idea you generate. In fact, when you brainstorm together, you may cocreate a solution that neither of you would have considered alone.

Nothing personal. Remember, this is just task conflict. Don't take anything personally, even if the discussion gets lively. If you do take something personally, it's time for a brave conversation to get you back on track with task conflict.

Mitigating Relationship Conflict

Relationship conflict is the conflict most of us think of when we think of conflict. It's the emotional, name-calling, judgment-filled conflict that most people dislike, and every family experiences it to one degree or another. Spend that much time with anyone, and relationship conflict is bound to emerge. It's human nature. Relationships go through cycles of rupture and repair.

Because relationship conflict amps up anxiety in most family systems, step one is to mitigate relationship conflict before it heightens. This helps to flush the anxiety from the system. Here are some strategies to de-escalate relationship conflict:

- **Focus on facts.** The more you are in conversation about the truth, the less you are in conversation using assumptions (which are often fear-based).

- **Use humor where appropriate.** Keeping things light relieves tension, promotes collaboration, and fosters creativity, which is helpful in generating ideas.
- **Disagree without being disagreeable.** The tone, intonation, and energy with which you communicate often matter more than the actual words. Keep your nonverbal communication positive and ensure your words, tone, and body language are in coherence. Speak with a shrewd head and a gentle heart.
- **Flatten hierarchy.** Create conditions for participants at every level (including family generations and business hierarchies) to feel safe enough to contribute their ideas. The most incisive solutions can come from knowledge-sharing across generations and hierarchies.
- **Fist to Five.** Borrowing from agile software development, Fist to Five[61] is a quick and effective way to assess consensus by voting. Because the group doesn't move forward until every person shows at least three fingers, nobody feels railroaded. Voting is decoded as follows:
    » **Closed fist** signals total opposition and an intent to prevent consensus.
    » **One finger** signals major concerns.
    » **Two fingers** signal a desire to discuss some minor issues.
    » **Three fingers** signal while not in total agreement, I am ready to move forward without further discussion.
    » **Four fingers** signal it's a good idea, and I will advocate for it.
    » **Five fingers** signal it's a great idea, and I want to lead it.
- **Make decisions provisional.** When participants are wary about committing to a solution, make the decision provisional by setting a date to revisit the decision. Reframe it as a "safe-to-fail" experiment from which family members simply gather data to learn more.

---

61 Andrew Zola, "fist to five (fist of five)" *Tech Target*, accessed March 2, 2024, https://www.techtarget.com/whatis/definition/fist-to-five-fist-of-five.

- **Yes . . . and.** Borrowed from improv, "Yes . . . and" is a way to carry the momentum forward, even when you disagree. The word "no" halts momentum, and most people dislike hearing it. "Yes . . . and" affirms a positive aspect of what you hear, then *adds to it* by saying "and" to introduce your perspective without negating the "yes." Examples:
    » *Yes*, I'm hungry too, *and* I'd like to find a restaurant that has more salad options.
    » *Yes*, building a bridge from one end of town to the other will eliminate stoplights, *and* we'll need to overcome funding, permit, and zoning hurdles.
    » *Yes*, Nelson works hard and deserves a raise, *and* let's discuss how to increase revenues or reduce expenses to find the budget for this.
    » *Yes*, I can see how you could interpret the email that way, *and* I hear it differently.

The most important word when using "yes . . . and" is the *and*. Most of us are accustomed to saying "Yes . . . but . . ." However, once you say "but," everything before the "but" is dismissed. It sounds the same as hearing "no." Compare "Yes, I can see how you could interpret the email that way, *but* I hear it differently," with "Yes, I can see how you could interpret the email that way, *and* I hear it differently."

If you find nothing that you can say *yes* to, then get curious. Assume the other person made the suggestion with good intentions, so find out what they are. For example, "Everything in me wants to say no to this idea, which makes me think I am missing something. What do you see as the upside of this approach?" Then actively listen to the point that you can paraphrase what you heard. You don't have to agree with it. Just understand it to the point that you can paraphrase it. "Yes . . . and" is one of the best communication hacks I know.

PRO TIP

Note that the conflict mitigation strategies in this chapter are all soft power strategies. Soft power allows others to retain agency and self-determination because soft power is an invitation, not a command. Soft power necessitates an openness to cocreation, learning, and not being right. It's enabling, trusting, generative, and supported by the belief that none of us is smarter than all of us. Soft power signifies respect for others as much as for self. Soft power is courageous and vulnerable because vulnerability takes courage, and courage necessitates vulnerability. They are two sides of the same coin.

Wise family business leaders use soft power even when they have access to the hard power associated with their business title or family hierarchy. They know that the game of family business is a game of hearts and minds, which aren't swayed by hard power.

If you feel tempted to exercise hard power, ask yourself if you are reacting to fear or exercising hard power from a place of love. If the origin is fear, exercise the EQ self-management techniques described in chapter 2 to manage your fear; then slow down and get some distance from the situation before deciding what approach to take next.

Paradoxically, research shows[62] that although empathy and social intelligence help us acquire power, once we acquire it, our empathy and social intelligence diminish. Therefore, remember that showing empathy, generosity, and authenticity doesn't come at the cost of highly competent, visionary leadership. You can embody both.

BOTTOM LINE: SMART IS BEING CLEVER ENOUGH TO WIN EVERY ARGUMENT. WISE IS BEING CLEVER ENOUGH NOT TO.

---

62 Lou Solomon, "Becoming Powerful Makes You Less Empathetic," *Harvard Business Review*, April 21, 2015, https://hbr.org/2015/04/becoming-powerful-makes-you-less-empathetic.

Brave Conversations to Work Through Relationship Conflict

The benefits of task conflict are much easier to reap when there's minimal relationship conflict simmering under the surface. However, when mitigating relationship conflict doesn't work, it's time to face it—because the only way past relationship conflict is *through* it.

Working through relationship conflict necessitates brave conversations, which, counterintuitively can *build* trust. Sure, the short-term emotional reactions of others may feel uncomfortable or awkward in the moment, but that discomfort can foster growth.

Although much has been published on how to have brave conversations,[63] I use this five-step process: PlayFAIR,[64] which stands for:

Permission
Facts
Assumptions
Impact
Request

Permission *"Do you have some time to talk? This should take about X minutes."*

Make sure you have enough time for the conversation and that both parties are prepared to engage. The right conversation at the wrong time is the wrong conversation. It's okay to share the topic if asked.

---

63 My favorite book on brave conversations is Shari Harley, *How To Say Anything To Anyone: A Guide to Building Business Relationships That Really Work*, (Austin: Greenleaf Book Group Press, 2013). Other books to support tough conversations include Susan Scott, *Fierce Conversations: Achieving Success at Work and in Life, One Conversation at a Time* (London: Penguin Publishing Group, 2004), and Kerry Patterson, Al Switzler, Joseph Grenny, Ron McMillan, *Crucial Conversations: Tools for Talking When Stakes Are High.* (New York: McGraw Hill, 2011).

64 You may be wondering why PlayFAIR instead of PFAIR? As a former client brilliantly pointed out, PlayFAIR is much easier to remember.

Facts *"I noticed that . . ."*

Start by stating the facts and only the indisputable facts. Starting with "I noticed . . ." implies a neutral observation. Be careful not to interpret the facts. For example, "You were short-tempered" is an assumption, not a fact. "Your voice grew louder, and your face reddened" is a fact.

Assumptions *"I'm telling myself that . . ."* or *"My story is . . ."*

Share your interpretation of the facts. This is the story you are telling yourself about the facts. It's important to "own" your story because it leaves room for other interpretations to coexist. Plus, if you state your story as "the truth," you may trigger defensiveness. Your goal is to keep egos to a minimum and curiosity to a maximum.

Impact *"The impact of this is . . ."*

State the relevant impact on you, others, and/or the organization to put it into a broader context. State what makes this important to address and watch your tone. Don't whine. Stay matter-of-fact to the extent appropriate.

Request *"I'd like to resolve this . . ."* or *"I have a request . . ."*

Express a desire to resolve the issue or make a request if you have one. Then *listen* with sincere curiosity to understand the other person's perspective. Paraphrase what you hear and ask, "Is that right?" until the other person affirms, "That's right." Remember, you don't have to agree with it to understand it.

PRO TIP

Active listening is critical to maintaining productive interpersonal relationships. Not taught in school, active listening necessitates curiosity and a focus on more than just words. It involves listening for tone and pace, watching body language, and getting curious about what is *not* said as much as what is.

Active listening involves listening with keen attention to the other person. The opposite of judgmental, active listening is being openly curious about another person's wants, needs, and feelings.

Highly skilled active listeners can listen without their own context getting in the way—their inner dialogue is quiet.

To improve your listening skills, start by paraphrasing what you heard. Skilled paraphrasers digest what they hear and share it back in their own words, allowing the other person to either confirm or correct their understanding with "Yes, that's right," or "No, let me explain it differently." Sometimes paraphrasing changes how the speaker understands their own situation. "Yes, you get it, but the way you said it made me think about it differently."

Paraphrasing lets the speaker know that they have been understood. This is important because humans have an innate craving to be seen, heard, understood, and valued, and paraphrasing gives the speaker a sense of exactly that. Until we *know* we have been heard, we tend not to listen to other points of view. Instead, we repeat the same point over and over. Don't undervalue paraphrasing to build connection when working through conflict, and remember that paraphrasing to reflect understanding does *not* imply that you agree. When I facilitate tense family meetings, I vigilantly invite participants to paraphrase what they heard before replying.

Even better than understanding another person's point of view is sensing how another person *feels* in their circumstances. The distinction between understanding someone cognitively and feeling genuine empathy is both subtle and meaningful. Often the first casualty in conflict, empathy is a bridge to understanding and connection, even if you wouldn't feel the same way given the same circumstances. In chapter 11 of David Brooks's book *How to Know a Person*, he describes the skills to cultivate and improve your empathy: mirroring, mentalizing, and caring.[65] This book is a terrific read for anybody who wants to strengthen their capacity to know others in a deeply meaningful way.

Active listening techniques include asking curious, open-ended

---

65   David Books, *How to Know a Person: The Art of Seeing Others Deeply and Being Deeply Seen,* (New York: Random House, 2023).

questions to learn more. Great curious questions often begin with "what" or "how," such as "What is at stake for you?" "How did you feel in that moment?" Poor curious questions are leading, such as "What if you just call him?"

Try to avoid questions that begin with "why" (such as "Why did you do that?") because it puts people on the defensive. Asking the same question but starting with "what," (such as "What motivated that?") sounds genuinely curious and less accusatory (assuming a neutral tone; tone matters.).

Silence, another active listening technique, allows both people in conversation to reflect and expand their thinking while in conversation. Although silence can feel socially awkward on occasion, experiment with it anyway.

Active listening takes practice. Start experimenting with active listening skills with a family member and notice how they respond. That could give you the courage to listen actively in more of your relationships.

BOTTOM LINE: STEPHEN COVEY SAID IT BEST: "SEEK FIRST TO UNDERSTAND, THEN TO BE UNDERSTOOD."

Inherent in the PlayFAIR approach is respect. Once respect is lost in a conversation, it's the only thing that matters. As Ron McMillan, coauthor of *Crucial Conversation*, writes, "Respect is like air. As long as it's present, nobody thinks about it. But if you take it away, it's all that people can think about. The instant people perceive disrespect in a conversation, the interaction is no longer about the original purpose—it is now about defending dignity."

These questions will help you prepare for a brave conversation:
- What outcome do you seek?
- What makes this important?
- What are the facts?

- What assumptions have you made?
- What assumptions might the other person hold?
- What do you want the other person to think or know?
- How do you want the other person to feel?
- What do you hope the other person will do?

Here's an example of a brave conversation. What used to sound like this . . .

"So help me, Madison, if you arrive late one more time, you're fired. You are an entitled brat, and you don't have any respect for me or this company. You don't deserve to work here."

. . . might sound like this instead:

"Madison, do you have some time to talk about work schedules? It should take about twenty minutes. Thanks for making time to talk. I noticed that you arrived at the office after 9:30 a.m. three times last week, and it's making me question your interest in the customer service role. When the department opens late, our brand promise of 'great quality service' gets questioned. I'm wondering . . . is there something going on that I'm not aware of?"

It could be that Madison's mother-in-law needed medical assistance this week. It could be that Madison has a second job and overslept. It could be that Madison has a substance abuse problem. Stay open-minded and openhearted so you don't make assumptions.

If this is the third time on the same topic, the request might change: "We've talked about this twice in the past, and I haven't seen any changes. I have a request: can you commit to being on time every day?" Note that there are only three possible responses to a clear request: yes, no, or a counteroffer. Once you have clarity and agreement on your request, you have the conditions for accountability.

If the behavior continues, the request may change again: "Madison, you have agreed to arrive on time every day, and you have been late twice this week already. It's time that we talk about whether this is the right role for you here, or whether this is even the right place for you to work. What can I do to help you find a role elsewhere? Because this isn't working for the customer service team." Because you have clarity and agreement, the conditions for accountability, you can draw your boundaries.

Once you have finished speaking, listen actively. Continue to assume good intent and listen to understand their perspective. Focus on your interests (high-functioning customer service) over your position (you're fired). Assess behavior, not the person. There's a canyon of difference between "you are entitled" and "that behavior is entitled."

After seeing the situation from the other person's lens, keep responsibility where it belongs. That means taking responsibility for anything that's yours to own and not taking responsibility for what's not. For example, when you promote your hardworking nephew over your niece, and your niece gets miffed, have a brave conversation with her, but don't feel guilty. That's "false guilt."[66] Your nephew earned the promotion.

As Melissa Mitchell-Blitch writes, "False guilt is true guilt's counterfeit. It feels the same—*bad*—as if to alert us we've done something wrong. But it occurs when we have done nothing wrong. In these situations, there is no corrective action to take, no lesson to learn. Thus false guilt can linger—for a long time—tormenting us with no evident means of escape. False guilt keeps us stuck in an emotional straitjacket until we recognize it for what it is and take off the straitjacket."

When Task Conflict Masquerades as Relationship Conflict

Some families are so uncomfortable with relationship conflict that they suffer endless task conflicts as a proxy war for relationship conflict. G2 siblings Rodney and Tonya have been avoiding conflict for four

---

66 Melissa Mitchell-Blitch, *In the Company of Family: How to Thrive When Business is Personal*, (Charleston: Eredita Consulting LLC, 2020).

decades. Each wants their own child to become CEO, and they have used their fiduciary board of directors as a proxy war battleground for their real issues. Tonya, confident a board-led succession process favors her child, strongly advocates for the board to lead CEO succession. Rodney, in contrast, lobbies to terminate the board, believing he has a greater chance of instating his child without a board in place. The existence of the board is the proxy fight for their real issue: timeworn sibling rivalry manifesting as whose child will lead the future. The endless board debate enables them to dodge the real conversation.

When relationship conflict masquerades as task conflict, you have a proxy war, so be honest about whether the conflict is personal or not; then choose your approach accordingly. If arguing about the logo color (which looks like task conflict) is the sandbox used to play out relationship conflict (such as a power struggle), don't follow the ALIGN process to address task conflict. That's bringing a knife to a gunfight. Have a PlayFAIR brave conversation instead.

Setting Boundaries

Brave conversations are often about setting and holding boundaries, which are important in both family relationships and business relationships. Brené Brown describes boundaries simply as what is okay and what is not okay. She says, "Daring to set boundaries is about having the courage to love ourselves even when we risk disappointing others."[67]

This is particularly hard in a family business because setting boundaries *can* disappoint others, and disappointing family violates the norms of the family mindset. Despite this, setting boundaries is an important skill to develop when working in a family business.

If setting a boundary provokes a negative response, remember that you are responsible for your own behavior, and others are responsible for theirs. The way people respond to you has more to do with them

---

67 "Brené Brown > Quotes > Quotable Quote," *goodreads*, accessed March 2, 2024. https://www.goodreads.com/quotes/8404453-daring-to-set-boundaries-is-about-having-the-courage-to-love.

than you. If they get angry, they are responsible for their anger. Perhaps their anger is masking a more vulnerable emotion such as fear, disappointment, embarrassment, or shame. Perhaps their anger is signposting a value that's at risk. Perhaps their reactivity reveals discomfort with a part of themselves they'd like to deny.

Most of us know when we feel angry. Few of us know when anger is masking a more vulnerable emotion. The more emotionally intelligent we are, the more honest we are with ourselves about the tender emotions that manifest as anger.

Contemplate this actual dialogue between siblings in their forties:

> **Lamont**: I recommend we use paper instead of plastic.
> **Shantae**: Plastic is cheaper and reusable.
> **Lamont**: I still prefer paper because it comes from a renewable source.
> **Shantae**: I've researched paper and plastic alternatives in great detail, and I'm telling you, plastic is the better option for this situation. Why do you even invite me to these meetings if you won't take my advice? There are more important things I could be doing with my time than attend these meetings.
> **Lamont**: #$@!%. This is a team effort! We need to work together! #$@!%. How dare you say that this isn't worth your time! You are such a #$@!%!!!

That's how conflict escalates. One sibling expresses irritation, and the other explodes—a familiar pattern of behavior between Lamont and Shantae. When Lamont and I debriefed the conversation later, we excavated more vulnerable emotions that lived underneath his anger. What he really felt was dismissed and scared that she thought he wasn't smart. It hurt his pride.

When I asked Lamont what holds him back from sharing that

truth with Shantae, he said, "I'm scared that if I share that honestly, I'll cry, and she will emotionally defeat me. I will lose whatever dignity I have left." That's why he gets angry. He feels boxed in. He can't speak his truth without losing face, so he explodes with anger in response to feeling dismissed and diminished by his sister.

PRO TIP

Instead of responding to anger with anger (which typically escalates conflict), respond with gentle curiosity instead. In *Balancing the Emotional Ledger*,[68] Joe Paul writes, "When you are dealing with an angry person, respond as if you are talking to a frightened person. People hide their fear behind anger because anger is a safer emotional state than fear, especially when one feels threatened. Speak as if you are talking to a person who is scared, and it will help the other person become more aware of what is actually threatening them."

Whether task conflict or relationship conflict, leaders who work *through* conflict have better business outcomes and happier work lives than those who avoid conflict for the sake of false harmony. In fact, working through conflict is key to family flourishing regardless of whether a business is involved. It's the family mindset's desire for harmony and the depth of the emotional roots that make it difficult.

PRO TIP

All families experience relationship conflict, and some families experience it to an extreme. The strategies above are helpful for common manifestations of conflict. If your family is experiencing deeply protracted conflict, seek support from someone skilled in complex facilitation. To assess the stage of conflict your family

---

68 Joe Paul, "Balancing the Emotional Ledger: Axioms and Guidelines for Counseling Families in Business," *Aspen Family Business Group*, https://www.aspenfamilybusiness.com/family-business-publications/bookstore/books/balancing-the-emotional-ledger.

may be experiencing, read Matthew Wesley's summary of a stages-of-conflict model created by Dr. Frederick Glasl, an Austrian economist, management consultant, and conflict researcher.[69]

Unsolvable (but Manageable) Conflict—Polarities

Last, some family business dilemmas are simply unsolvable because they are not a problem that has a solution; they are a tension that needs to be managed. In earlier chapters, we've explored some common family business polarities that spur conflict, including:

- Invest :: harvest (as related to dividends)
- Inherit :: merit (as related to ownership succession)
- Reveal :: conceal (as related to estate planning)

These dilemmas are complex, adaptive challenges that require a different mindset to work through. This mindset is so important that it has its own chapter. Chapters 9 and 10 are devoted to *how* to manage these polarities, to ease conflict born from an unsolvable paradox.

Before we get there, however, let's look at how the family :: business polarity affects family business succession in chapter 7 and family business governance in chapter 8. Spoiler alert, succession and governance in a family business are nothing like succession and governance in a public corporation. We'll start with succession.

---

69 For a summary of stages of family conflict, read this blog post from Matthew Wesley, "The Levels of Conflict: A Diagnostic Approach," *Family Wealth*, May 20, 2013, https://www.thewesleygroup.com/blog/?p=404.

Questions for Chapter 6

1. What brave conversations are you avoiding? For the sake of what?
2. In conflict, what is your automatic response? Fight, flight, freeze, or fawn?
3. Does your family business culture lean more toward conflict-avoidant or conflict seeking? Is the family culture leaning too far in one way or the other?
4. What is the review/feedback process for family employees? How do you support their growth and development?
5. When is being nice causing harm? What would being kind look or sound like?
6. How trustworthy are you in these six areas: fairness, honesty, forgiveness, reliability, vulnerability, and forthright communication? Where could you improve?
7. How do you discern when to mitigate relationship conflict and when to work through relationship conflict?
8. What brave conversations are missing?
9. Where do you need to set better boundaries?

"A king, realizing his incompetence, can either delegate or abdicate his duties. A father can do neither. If only sons could see the paradox, they would understand the dilemma."

—Marlene Dietrich

CHAPTER 7
RESOLVING COMMON DILEMMAS IN LEADERSHIP SUCCESSION

"*Son, you have twenty-four hours to decide whether to partner with me.*" *Still foggy from celebrating his twenty-sixth birthday the night before, Breck wasn't expecting his father's call. "I have an idea," said his father, Eugene, who proceeded to pitch an intriguing business idea. Breck had twenty-four hours to decide whether to join him.*

The following day, Breck called Eugene and said yes. By October, he and Eugene had cofounded a business split 51 percent father/49 percent son. The business concept was sound, and it quickly grew to $25M in annual sales.

For fifteen years, Breck loved working with his dad. They were not immune to the typical ego challenges in a family business . . . Breck occasionally competed with his father, trying to prove he was better, faster, smarter. As Eugene edged closer to retirement, he grew more risk averse, whereas Breck wanted to experiment with new ideas and take bigger risks. Strategic reinvestment discussions were predictably tense but not abnormally so.

The real issues didn't surface until year sixteen when Eugene started to slow down. Eugene shortened his workweek to twenty-five hours while retaining his full-time salary, and Breck began to fear that Eugene was putting the business in jeopardy. For four years, Breck's resentment grew and grew until Breck gave his father an ultimatum: "Sell me the business, or I leave," said Breck. "You have eighteen months to decide."

The subsequent eighteen months destroyed their relationship.

By then, the business had stagnated, exacerbating the tension between father and son. Concerned about their retirement, Eugene's wife (Breck's stepmother) urged Eugene to push for a higher valuation of the business for the buyout. Eugene withered under the intense pressure from both his wife and son.

The stress turned Breck into a different man, one seething with rage and certainly not the father or husband he wanted to be. He desperately wanted to leave, but the family mindset left him "riddled with guilt, obligation, and self-doubt. The decision to leave the family business took me a year to get to," he continued. "It's extremely hard to leave. If you are in a corporate setting and you are dissatisfied with your work or boss, you put your résumé out and begin again. Not so in a family business."

Then, eighteen months to the day after Breck's ultimatum, the phone rang. "I've signed the papers," Eugene said. "The business is yours." A flood of surprise, relief, and sadness flooded his body as Breck hung up the phone.

Within two years, the business was thriving again, but Breck's relationship with his father never fully recovered. And last week, Breck's ten-year-old son announced to his father, "Daddy, I will be running your company someday."

◆ ◆ ◆

The mere presence of the family mindset makes the succession process for family-led businesses distinctly different from the corporate succession familiar to the business mindset.

First, leadership succession occurs far less frequently in a family business than in a large corporation. Whereas family-operated businesses typically change leaders once per generation, the average tenure for the CEO of a public company is six years.[70]

Second, family-led businesses choose their successors from within a small group of family members. In contrast, internal succession in a public company begins with a talent assessment tool called a "9-Box," which assesses talent in a matrix with *performance* on one axis and *potential* on the other. External succession might begin with an executive search firm to source potential successors from the marketplace.

Third, unlike public companies, family business succession involves both leadership *and* ownership succession, which aren't necessarily concurrent. Both types of succession can feel especially tumultuous due to the ensuing renegotiation of power, especially when a transition is unexpected or poorly planned. The stakes are high because decisions made in the short run can set the precedent for the long run. Of course, that doesn't have to be the case, but renegotiating after the fact can be harder.

Ultimately, family business succession rests on myriad sub-polarities in addition to the meta family mindset :: business mindset polarity. Breck's story illustrates two common polarities in family business succession. If the tension is sooner :: later for the leading generation, the tension is urgent :: patient for the rising generation. This chapter explores these succession tensions.

Sooner :: Later

The leading generation's notorious struggle is sooner :: later. Some generation leaders can't pass the torch fast enough, eager for the rising generation to accept the responsibilities of leadership whether they are prepared or not. Other generation leaders die with their boots on. Rarely is there a Goldilocks transition that supports thoughtful business continuity.

---

70   George Stalk, Jr. and Henry Foley, "Avoid the Traps That Can Destroy Family Businesses," *Harvard Business Review*, January-February 2012.

Sooner

Early succession, when unplanned, can overwhelm rising-generation leaders, especially when they step into considerable power at a young age. Power can be heady. Research[71] has shown that when people gain power, their empathy decreases, as does their ability to read other people's emotions, two key components of emotional intelligence. This matters because EQ accounts for almost 90 percent of what sets high-performing leaders apart from peers with similar technical skills and knowledge.[72]

At twenty-three, Arnold became CEO when his father died unexpectedly. Consistent with his Filipino heritage, he became the instant patriarch, working with his mother, brother, and sister. As he describes it, "I'm the oldest, and now I'm the patriarch, so I make the calls," said Arnold. "If I tell my sister something needs to be fixed, even if she doesn't agree, she won't talk back to me. Same with my brother. He won't come against me because of our Filipino culture."

Aware of his power, he doesn't worry about hurting their feelings. "Nothing can be questioned by my family. Nobody tells me what to do." But this isolation from feedback pleases and frustrates Arnold. "It's both good and bad to have this freedom. It's difficult for me to discipline myself. Time management gets difficult. I always have a plan, but it never works out that way. As patriarch, I never know when I'm messing up."

Nobody speaks truth to power in Arnold's family, leaving him without the benefits of other perspectives. Leaders with disproportionate power, given their age and experience, can greatly benefit from mentors and coaches to support them in their leadership journeys.

In the sooner :: later polarity, this succession happened too soon. Arnold wasn't mature enough to handle the power he inherited after the sudden loss of his father.

---

71 Dacher Keltner, *Berkeley Psychology*, accessed March 3, 2024, https://psychology.berkeley.edu/people/dacher-keltner.
72 Daniel Goleman, "What Makes a Leader?" *Harvard Business Review*, January 2004.

<u>Later</u>

Although some leaders assume power too early, more legendary is the leader who cedes power too late. Turning sixty seems to prompt leaders to craft a five-year transition plan for the rising generation, but the operative word here is *plan*. Although the plan starts out as a five-year plan, it often stays a five-year plan indefinitely. When the leader turns sixty, the plan is to retire at sixty-five. Then at sixty-five, the plan is to retire at seventy. At seventy . . . you get the picture.

Nevertheless, continually postponing retirement makes perfect sense when you worry:
- Will I lose my power if I step down?
- Is my successor capable? Will she take care of my employees?
- How do I transfer decades of knowledge to a new leader?
- What happens to my retirement if my successor can't pay off the loan I made to buy me out?
- What if the note payments to pay off the loan thwart needed reinvestments in the business?
- Will my successor be better than me? Will I look like a fool?
- What will I *do* (and who will I *be*?) when I'm not the leader of the business?
- How will my friends view me?
- How will being around the house affect my marriage?
- What else could give me the joy, purpose, and relevance that leading the family business gives me?
- I've heard about people who retired and died within a year . . . I'm not ready to die!

These worries reveal the understandable competing commitments that make transitioning the business to the rising generation unappealing at best and terrifying at worst. Many leaders also *assume* that a business transition will turn these concerns into a reality. Until those assumptions are tested, leaders who favor *later* in the sooner ::

later polarity are loath to release power.

Sven (G3 CEO, age seventy-seven) isn't stepping down despite appreciating how his father transitioned leadership by "giving me lots of autonomy to learn and grow." After taking over at thirty-five, Sven spent the next forty-plus years growing the business from eighty employees to over 4,000. But when asked about his own retirement, Sven simply replies, "Inconceivable."

Succession in a family business is as much an emotional process as an intellectual one. Family members, consultants, and *Harvard Business Review* can list all the brilliant reasons why a family business should engage in a thoughtful succession plan. Purposefully planned leadership continuity is in the best interests of the family and the business, but it doesn't stand a chance against a leader who has competing commitments with such deep emotional roots.

Given advancements in health care, retirement in the baby boomer generation looks quite different from retirement in prior generations. Fifty years ago, retirement expectations were five to seven years. Today, retirees are likely to experience several decades of healthy activity, which is surfacing new challenges.

When a leader's identity is fused with her business, passing the baton to the rising generation can be dreadful. That loss of identity can feel like being stripped of your clothing in the cold wilderness. Without a new identity to embrace, it's no wonder leaders maintain a vice grip on power. It takes courage to transition from an identity one has known and enjoyed during adult life, especially in a family business where pride in your role is connected to pride in your family.

Although retirement from a public corporation can trigger anxiety, stepping down from leading a *family business* feels different due to the personal, familial connection. The business can feel like an extension of themselves, making succession that much more difficult.

Trent, our forty-six-year-old G4 CEO introduced in chapter 5, sees it similarly. "With no succession plan in place, it's hugely damaging to a family business," he said. "Previous generations hang on way too long. That's why family businesses don't last. The new generation needs to take over to survive."

Leaders who are unable to release power can thwart potential. Fresh leadership can foster much-needed innovation and challenge sacred cows that prior leaders refused to address. New leaders can rejuvenate a workforce and introduce new energy to motivate the team.

Thomas (also G4 CEO) is grateful for how his father thoughtfully transferred leadership to him. "Dad never looked over my shoulder and second-guessed me," especially after watching his grandfather transfer the business to his dad. "Grandpa never let go," said Thomas. "Grandpa would call from Florida every morning, asking questions for up to two hours. It made my dad crazy. One day, he broke down crying because he couldn't handle it anymore. It was emotionally disastrous." Succession between generations can be just plain hard.

Rising generation leaders with high emotional intelligence know to honor the leading generation's need for relevance and recognition before, during, and after succession. Gary (age sixty, CEO, in-law) struggled to succeed his father-in-law at first, even though his father-in-law had handpicked Gary over his own three children.

"My father-in-law recruited me into the business twenty times before I finally joined, but I struggled as an outsider to contribute," said Gary. "The more progress I made, the more offensive it was to him because it implied that the old regime wasn't good. Nobody gave me a book to figure that out, but I eventually did. For the last ten of my thirty-four years in the business, I've had a wonderful relationship with my father-in-law because I realized that my job wasn't just to grow the business. One of my primary objectives was to give him relevance." With his ego in check, Gary played the long game.

After a few bumpy years, Gary navigated the sooner :: later polarity beautifully by confidently taking the reins of the business and honoring his father-in-law's emotional need for relevance. That's how to navigate a polarity . . . develop strategies that acquire the upsides of both ends of the pole.

PRO TIP

Although perfectly rational, strategic, and wise for family businesses to document a robust succession plan, statistics show that most family businesses do not have one in place.[73] Because sooner or later, succession *will* occur, be sure to *at least* document an emergency succession plan in the case of unplanned succession. Then set a date for when and how you will design a longer-term, purposeful succession plan.

Urgent :: Patient

The rising-generation manages a different tension: urgent :: patient. Fueling the angst of the rising generation are a different set of worries, such as

- When will I get to lead? I have so many ideas I am dying to put into place.
- What if my parents (aunts/uncles) refuse to step back? How long do I have to wait?
- Am I better off leaving the family business or staying put?
- What if I fail? It's my last name, after all, that qualified me for this job.
- How will I afford to buy this company, especially since my parents' retirement is dependent on what I pay?
- How will my siblings (and cousins) feel about me being the leader of our shared asset?

These worries reveal the understandable competing commitments that make assuming leadership responsibilities from the leading generation unsettling. Although many rising-generation family members are quite comfortable waiting for the leading generation to pass the

---

73   PwC's 2023 US Family Business Survey, *PwC*, May 16, 2023, accessed March 3, 2024, https://www.pwc.com/us/en/services/trust-solutions/private-company-services/library/family-business-survey.html.

torch, most rising-generation leaders favor urgency over patience.

Gunther (age thirty-seven, G2 president) was desperate to restructure the shop floor and replace key people in the business his father started, but his father was "convinced the only fix is to work harder and longer," said Gunther. "Dad resists change, but it's still my problem," Gunther continued, feeling simultaneously responsible and powerless. "Dad is in the weeds, and it's difficult to talk about that with him," Gunther says. "I'm trying to create the least amount of friction, so I internalize stuff. There's anxiety, frustration. It's crushing." With deference to elders born from the family mindset, Gunther internalizes the pressure and suffers in silence.

Gunther described succession as the single most challenging aspect of a family business. At sixty-eight, his father is not ready to let go. "My dad isn't willing to discuss it," says Gunther. "I don't know what will happen with this business." So Gunther waits quietly, growing more anxious every year.

According to Harry Levinson, a psychologist who pioneered the application of psychology to leadership, parent-child rivalry can tear families apart and is particularly difficult on the child.[74] "The father looks on the son as ungrateful and unappreciative, and the son feels both hostile to his father and guilty for his hostility," he writes.

Some in the rising generation wait patiently, loyal to their parent, for their chance in the sun. Many contemplate leaving, but instead, they stay, convinced that leaving would mean passing up an opportunity that is almost within their reach. That pressure can build over time, generating disappointment, frustration, and resentment and sometimes permanently harming family relationships.

Although there's no formula to solve the sooner :: later polarity, the polarity framework in chapters 9 and 10 supports individuals and families to have the necessary conversations and design the both/and strategies that harmonize the benefits of sooner *and* later.

---

74 Harry Levinson, "Conflicts That Plague Family Businesses," *Harvard Business Review*, March 1971.

Let's revisit seventy-seven-year-old Sven, who considers retirement inconceivable. What does he want? If Sven's goal is to live a fulfilled, satisfied life, then he's doing that just beautifully. However, if Sven wants the business to thrive for generations to come, what is the consequence of retaining power? How can he prepare the rising generation for leadership if he doesn't give them a chance to develop? Recall the me :: we polarity introduced in chapter 1? Sven's lopsided focus on his own needs (me) may hamper the business (we).

What a privilege it would be for Sven's successor to develop as a leader while Sven is around to provide a sounding board for decision-making. He could reshape his identity from magnate to mentor, in favor of a longer-term family goal over his short-term self-actualization. Not every leader can see how their legacy is more secure and long-lasting when transitions are thoughtfully planned.

In another example of a leader favoring later over sooner, Jason (G4 vice president) may himself retire before his eighty-four-year-old mother steps down. Famously controlling, she keeps any threats to her power at bay. "Mom makes every major decision at this company," he said. "At fifty-four years old, I have virtually no authority and no respect from the employees of this company."

With his mother's health starting to fade, he is growing more concerned about the impact on the business. He will become the CEO when his mother passes, and "the employees are scared of what will happen when she dies. They haven't seen me with any responsibility, and Mom isn't doing anything to prepare me or the company for a healthy leadership transition," said Jason.

Jason is full of ideas to improve the business, "but Mom disagrees with every idea I suggest," he laments. "I love my mother and have obeyed her wishes for decades, but she's going to leave me this business in tatters." Jason wouldn't think of leaving his family business but feels powerless to effect change. This family has missed the Goldilocks zone for a successful leadership transition and will surely suffer the overuse of *later* at the cost of *sooner*.

PRO TIP

Here are some questions to help the leading generation think through the long-term impacts of delaying succession:

- What would you do differently if you renamed "succession planning" to "business continuity planning?"
- What is your greatest hope for the *business* in twenty years?
- What is your greatest hope for the *family* in twenty years?
- Now imagine it *is* twenty years in the future, and you have realized your greatest hopes for your family and your business. Looking back, what did you do (and not do) over the past twenty years to achieve those great outcomes?
- Now imagine it is still twenty years in the future, but your family and/or your business has struggled. Looking back, what did you do (and not do) over the past twenty years that led to these disappointing outcomes?
- What will happen if you keep doing what you've always done?

BOTTOM LINE: IF YOU NEED TO MAKE DECISIONS ABOUT SUCCESSION BUT KEEP AVOIDING THEM, ENGAGE WITH A COACH OR THERAPIST TO SUPPORT YOUR UNDERSTANDING OF WHAT'S REALLY AT PLAY.

Tradition :: Innovation

Leadership transitions can trigger cultural tensions between generations, especially between tradition and innovation. Typically, the rising generation favors innovation, whereas the leading generation favors tradition (but not always).

Both extremes cause problems. A lopsided focus on tradition ("but we've always done it this way") can lead to obsolescence. Buggy whips were a big business before the invention of the automobile. Streaming services destroyed Blockbuster. Conversely, a disproportionate focus on innovation can lead to failure due to unprofitable gambles on unproven technologies and dwindling funds for reinvestment in the core business.

Either way, change can be hard for both generations. The rising generation can lose patience with the leading generation, who misses a window of opportunity with new technology, while competitors benefit from early adoption. And the leading generation can feel passed over and irrelevant when the rising generation pushes for change.

Trent struggled to drive change when he took the reins from his father and uncles. "What I find most challenging in leading a family business is dealing with my dad and the previous generation's way of doing things," said Trent. "Technology is increasing the pace of change, and I had to break the previous generation's preconceived notions of how we get things done."

After five years of unsuccessful attempts to modernize, the resistance to technology became an impediment, so Trent quit. He wrote his dad "a Dear John letter and let it all hang out," but his mom intercepted the letter before it reached his father. She called Trent and said, "I know it's bad. I saw your letter. Let me keep Dad in Florida for three months." By the time his father returned, Trent had upgraded the entire technology infrastructure. "Mom basically forced Dad into retirement," acknowledges Trent. "And to this day, I don't know if Mom ever showed Dad my letter." Trent's mom used her shadow influence to ease her husband into retirement and set her son up to modernize the business. Her use of soft power set both men up for success.

Similarly, the change Paula (from chapter 2) introduced was painful for her parents to endure. "Succession from my mother to me was difficult for everyone because it came with a culture change as well," said Paula. "The old culture was 'command and control,' and we had a victim mentality." When Paula took over, she distributed decision authority to the appropriate departments and upended the victim mindset.

"I made it clear that we are in control; we are not victims of circumstance," she said. "We have choices and therefore responsibility.

The victim mindset from the prior generation allowed us to give up responsibility. I changed that," she said with pride. Innovation doesn't always show up as a new product or service. Sometimes a culture change is the innovation the business needs.

The Family Mindset and Women in Business

Women tend to assume positions of power sooner in family businesses than women in large corporations, courtesy of the family mindset. When coveted ownership and leadership positions are held for family members, demographics play a role since women make up about 50 percent of the rising generations. Recent studies have shown that women in family businesses are 70 percent more likely to serve in top management positions than women in corporations.[75]

Unfortunately, the business mindset doesn't always make it easy for women, since patriarchy is still embedded within it. The CEO of her grandfather's highly profitable manufacturing business, Paula struggled on her way to the C-Suite. She joined the business at twenty-two, filled with spunk, confidence, and intellect, but when she identified areas for improvement to her boss, the nonfamily production manager, "He patronized, ignored, and belittled me," said Paula. She pointed out the same problems to her father and older brother, "but even they wouldn't listen. And if they did, they were louder and more experienced debaters, so they would shut me down. I would just cry," she said.

Frustrated and humiliated, Paula almost quit multiple times, but her tenacity and determination kept her there. "I come from a fiercely competitive family, so when I heard 'you can't,' I thought, *Just watch me!*" Had she been treated that way in a nonfamily business, she would have resigned, but the commitment to family enabled her to dig deep and find grit.

Over time, her emotional intelligence improved. She trained herself to walk away when she needed time to gather her thoughts, enhancing her ability to manage her emotions and deal with facts.

---

75   Joe Astrachan, Ph.D., Torsten M. Pieper, Ph.D., Marnix van Rij and Carrie Hall, "Women in Leadership: The Family Business Advantage," *EY*, 2017.

"Eleven years later, my father fired the production manager, and his house of cards came crashing down." For years, the production manager had been covering up the misdeeds to which Paula had been pointing, and her family finally saw it. Vindication at last!

By age forty, Paula had matured as a leader, and her father chose Paula over Paula's brother to be the next CEO. As proud of herself as she was as a professional, she was equally pained as a sister because she knew how disappointed her brother felt. "Grandpa told my brother that *he* would be CEO someday," she admitted. The rules of the family mindset (love and support your family) conflicted with the rules of the business mindset (compete and win).

PRO TIP

Paula experienced a common emotion in family businesses: false guilt.[76] She didn't do anything wrong, but knowing her brother felt passed over because of her success made her feel responsible for his emotional suffering. Her promotion violated traditional social norms: sons succeed their fathers, and daughters collaborate, not compete. When you notice yourself feeling guilt, ask yourself if you would (or even could) do anything differently. If you recognize true guilt, acknowledge your mistake and make amends. If there's nothing you did or said, then release the false guilt. It's not yours to own.

The Family Mindset and Young Leaders

Family businesses can also provide early leadership opportunities for the rising generation, opportunities corporate leaders wouldn't think of offering to workers in their twenties. Although exciting, assuming substantial leadership positions at a young age can be

---

[76] Melissa Mitchell-Blitch, *In the Company of Family: How to Thrive When Business is Personal*, (Charleston: Eredita Consulting LLC, 2020), Mitchell-Blitch, Melissa. *In the Company of Family: How to Thrive When Business is Personal*. Charleston: Eredita Consulting LLC, 2020. 79-86.

intimidating because sometimes these opportunities are given based on family lineage, not readiness.

Rising-generation leaders can feel like frauds when they question whether they earned their title based on merit or birthright. Some respond to that self-doubt with a fierce desire to prove their worth. Others respond with a lethargy that others perceive as "entitled." Some recognize that both may be true—their title is a function of both merit and birthright—and it's okay.

Ava, from chapter 4, took over her family's construction business in her twenties, following the unexpected death of her father. Although she experienced self-doubt in the early years, she learned to trust her leadership instincts, and the business is thriving thirty years later. "There was a lot of pressure when my dad died," she said. "I was in my twenties and suddenly responsible for this business that my great-grandfather started." Ava said, "If I keep moving and keep making decisions, nobody will know that I don't know what I'm doing." Five to ten years later, she learned that her instincts were better than she thought, and she hasn't looked back.

Unexpected, early leadership can be a two-edged sword. When flung into the deep end of the pool, some leaders, like Ava, learn to swim. But with others, the self-doubt lingers, leaving many wondering if their skills have value outside the family business. "Working in the family business offered me a unique experience to get in over my head," said Gunther. "But how transferable I am to the open market? That, I've never been able to gauge," he wondered. "I'm thirty-seven, and I don't have a degree or experience, so I can't walk into someplace new." That constrained sense of agency can weigh heavily when times are bad. Gunther lacked confidence that he could earn a sufficient wage outside the family business, which left him in a dilemma—unhappy if he stayed, unable to support himself if he left.

Spencer, from chapter 2, pressured himself to earn respect by demonstrating high competence. "The biggest challenge I face is 'the owner's son' stigma. It doesn't matter how good you are or how hard you work. You achieved this because of who you are, not your ability," said Spencer. "At a very young age, I had responsibilities no sane person would take on."

Spencer dwelled on how he was perceived. "It wasn't easy to get the respect of the few people who worked for my family. It was hard to motivate people. They don't buy in because of ability; they buy in due to obligation. Even the people I hired, over time . . . I wondered what they really thought!" lamented Spencer. "It's hard to tell who is sucking up, who was working in good faith, and who is blowing smoke." Spencer recognized that these fears were in his head. "A lot of this is self-imposed . . . you doubt yourself," he said.

His initial self-confidence waned over time. "After college, I had confidence in my natural abilities, based on projects I took on at a young age. Joining the family business seemed like the best opportunity to grow." But he wonders if he joined too early. "Maybe if I had come in after five years from someplace else, I'd feel like I had more respect from people. I suffered from so much self-doubt, so much frustration!" Spencer didn't realize how much respect he had earned until he sold the business. The new owners kept him on for years after his contract ended.

Self-doubt is common, even *with* work experience outside of the family business. Yannick, from chapter 1, doubted himself despite five years at a Fortune 100 firm and an MBA before joining his family business. Fortunately, he was aware of his self-talk and put it into perspective, especially when he reflected on his compensation and realized that he'd consistently earned the first or second largest bonus in his department. "My advice?" he said. "Don't be afraid to own a family business, but be aware of the self-doubt that comes with it."

As a young leader, managing nonfamily employees can feel uncomfortable. Liza became vice president of her growing family business at thirty-four but felt awkward managing the more tenured staff. "We've had some people here forever," she said. "My first kiss in first grade was with our CFO's son. He's been around since I was born. It's really hard to conduct performance reviews with someone who used to change your diapers," she acknowledged sheepishly.

Similarly, Gunther Haugen, G2 president, feels an uncomfortable distance between himself and his employees, many of whom have been working for his family's business for three decades. "If you work for Haugen Enterprises and your last name is Haugen, people treat you differently," he said. "For example, I have an awkward relationship with the engineering manager. When I ask him questions about design, he doesn't think I know what I'm talking about. But he gets lost in the weeds, and I'm good at the big-picture stuff," says Gunther. "He needs to understand the direction we're going. Part of the family business issue is that we have employees who have been here for almost thirty years. I'm thirty-seven, and I grew up with them, but now I'm telling them how to do stuff. It's awkward."

Sometimes nonfamily leaders are surprised and disappointed when senior roles in a family business are reserved for family members. They often fail to recognize the impact of the family mindset in succession and cling to the business mindset's rule of meritocracy. Driven by resentment for being passed over, some try to sabotage the family leader. Others leave to work for a nonfamily business that will recognize and reward them according to traditional business norms. The nonfamily leaders who shine replace their "Hey, what about me?" mindset with "What can I do to support this family leader so we all thrive?"

It's no surprise that tenured employees bring a skeptical eye to family members who are invited into leadership positions prematurely by traditional business standards. It's hard on both the employees who question the credibility of the family leader and the family leader who strives to earn the respect of her team. In situations like this, improving one's emotional intelligence is helpful to family and nonfamily leaders alike.

Other Succession Polarities

In addition to the sooner :: later, urgent :: patient, and tradition :: innovation polarities, other succession polarities tend to crop up during ownership and leadership succession.

The equal :: fair polarity is especially prevalent in ownership succession when some descendants work in the business and some do not. Take Brady, the thirty-eight-year-old G2 president of his parent's business. Ever since Brady joined the business eight years ago, his parents have gifted each of their three children equal shares, but only Brady works there. His siblings don't. Further, under Brady's leadership, the business has grown from a cozy, twenty-person shop into an eighty-person (and growing) highly reputable and profitable firm.

Believing equal is fair, his parents were transferring a third of the business to each child, which irked Brady. With only a third ownership, he'd need at least one sibling's approval to make any major decisions about the business, given neither sibling worked there. That felt risky. Plus, the business was rapidly becoming his parents' greatest asset under Brady's leadership, and he objected to putting in the blood, sweat, and tears needed to grow the business while earning only a third of the spoils. It just didn't feel fair.

Brady had a brave conversation with this parents, and fortunately, they understood his point of view. So did Brady's siblings. The family decided to change the estate plan to give Brady more than 50 percent of the business (and equalize the siblings with other assets). Then, they lined up responsibilities with privileges and brought the siblings onto the board of directors so they were informed about the business and could actively support its continued growth. Everyone in the family is satisfied with this change. That's not the only path they could have settled on. Other solutions could have harmonized the family mindset and business mindset just as well.

As unique as succession is in a family business, so is governance. The next chapter, chapter 8, explores common governance polarities, and chapters 9 and 10 are dedicated to how to navigate the tensions resulting from these polarities.

Questions for Chapter 7

For Leading Generation:
1. When you think about business continuity, what excites you? What concerns you?
2. What leadership transition strategies would serve the needs of the business best? The family best? Both the business and the family?
3. How will you know when the rising generation is ready to take on more responsibility? Be specific.
4. What alternatives can you explore if the rising generation isn't interested or able to assume leadership?
5. Who will you be in your third act, when you're no longer leading your family business? What will bring you meaning and purpose?
6. Do you favor tradition or innovation? What do you fear most about the other?

For Rising Generation:
1. What values does the leading generation offer, and how will you retain those values when you take over? What values will you leave behind? What new values will you introduce?
2. How will your leadership be similar to that of your predecessor? Different?
3. How will you know when you are ready to lead? Be specific.
4. How long are you willing to wait to lead the business? What alternatives do you have?
5. How can you help the retiring leader stay relevant?
6. Do you favor tradition or innovation? What do you fear most about the other?

"Freedom is not the last word. Freedom is only part of the story and half of the truth. Freedom is but the negative aspect of the whole phenomenon whose positive aspect is responsibleness. In fact, freedom is in danger of degenerating into mere arbitrariness unless it is lived in terms of responsibleness. That is why I recommend that the Statue of Liberty on the East Coast be supplemented by a Statue of Responsibility on the West Coast." [77]

—VIKTOR FRANKL

---

77 Alex Pattagos, Ph.D., "Viktor Frankl and the Statue of Responsibility: Balancing Freedom and Responsibility," *Psychology Today*, August 8, 2019, accessed March 4, 2024, https://www.psychologytoday.com/us/blog/the-meaningful-life/201908/viktor-frankl-and-the-statue-responsibility

CHAPTER 8
RESOLVING THE COMMON DILEMMAS IN FAMILY BUSINESS GOVERNANCE

Lorenzo's Story

"Never in my sixty-seven years on this earth have I struggled with a business decision as much as this one," said Lorenzo, G2 chairman, his head lowered while he spoke with his attorney. "Should I pass ownership of the business to my children as fifty-fifty co-owners, or should I split the business into two different entities and give one to each child? It looks like either option will destroy our family."

Lorenzo's daughter, Sofia, age forty, managed the retail side of the business, but that's not where they made their money. The profits came from the wholesale side, which Paulo, his thirty-seven-year-old son, led. Paulo's head for business impressed Lorenzo.

Because the original plan was for Sofia and Paulo to own the business together, Lorenzo, Sofia, and Paulo had spent the last eighteen months with a top family business governance consultant finalizing their family business governance policies. For months, his children bickered about the details.

Lorenzo turned to his attorney, concern chiseling deep into his brow.

"If we remain together as a family business, Paulo will explode. He doesn't need Sofia or the retail side, and he's sick to death of slowing down for her," he said." However, if we separate assets, Sofia will implode. She needs Paulo to be successful, and if left alone, she'd blow through her inheritance in a few years. No matter which decision I make, I will alienate one of my children. What should I do?"

Paulo's Story

After weeks of haggling over an organizational chart, Sofia finally agreed to the latest draft of governance documents, with one condition: "We work on our communication."

"Communication?" Paulo lost it. He had provided report after report after report, and still, it was not enough for Sofia. "The brain damage is unending," said Paulo. "I am carrying this business for the entire family. I'm the one generating the profits, and I'm doing it for her children as much as for my own. Does she want me to inform her every time I staple a document? How much more can I communicate than I already do?"

Feeling a heavy burden of responsibility for the family, Paulo intuitively understood that their father wanted Paulo to keep the business profitable for both Paulo and Sofia. But he was furious that Sofia's top priority had been to increase her salary and *her ownership distributions. "Every penny we pay out in compensation is a penny we are not reinvesting in the business. She earns more than enough. . . . What more does she want?"*

What gigs him the most, however, is the implication that Paulo isn't trustworthy. Why else would she want more communication? he wonders. *Paulo acts with impeccable integrity, so when she questions his communication in light of his work ethic, it infuriates him.*

Sofia's Story

Sofia lobbied hard for an increase in pay. "I have three kids, and they are all attending private schools," she said. "Plus, life is expensive. Our country club membership dues just went up again!" Now that she has negotiated the income she wants, for now at least, she is ready to understand the details of the governance proposals.

"It took me a while to understand these documents, but after speaking with my attorney, I finally understand and am ready to agree to everything, as long as Paulo works on his communication," she announced. "I want to be able to walk into the office on Monday mornings and ask how his weekend went without getting the cold shoulder. He is so hostile to me. He crosses his arms, furrows his brow, and refuses to make eye contact. How can I have a civil, much less business, relationship with someone with such poor interpersonal skills? I need him to work on the fundamentals of communication before I sign anything."

◆ ◆ ◆

Sofia and Paulo lived on the opposite ends of a responsibility :: privileges polarity, and it skewed how they viewed each other. Where Paulo saw Sofia as an entitled spendthrift who intentionally obstructed progress, Sofia saw Paulo as an uptight, arrogant skinflint who spoke to her with disrespect. Although close as children, they now irritated each other, leaving their father, Lorenzo, feeling boxed in. He cared deeply for both children and agonized that their growing discord would rip the family apart.

Governance Polarities

This story introduces the concept of family business governance—a decision structure that is quite different from governance in other kinds of organizations. If you already understand family business governance basics or it's not relevant to you at this time, skip to chapters 9 and 10, the most important chapters of this book. For convenience, I've included an appendix that explains common terminology in family business governance, such as family constitution, family charter, family council, etc.

At its most basic, governance is "deciding how to decide," and it provides the checks and balances needed to manage the tensions in the family :: business polarity. Especially useful in managing the tension in the privileges :: responsibilities polarity, governance defines the *process* for who, when, and how decisions are made. Good governance mitigates conflict because it defines, in advance, the process for making decisions, and in most family businesses, *fairness about the process supersedes fairness about the outcome*. Last, good governance ensures that the right people are making the right decisions at the right time.

Let's start with some simple stories that exemplify common polarities in family business governance. Chapters 9 and 10 will show you how to navigate them successfully.

Top Down :: Bottom Up

When Sue and Bob sold their family business, they started a foundation with a clear mission to rescue dogs and cats and a hidden hope that it would keep their children connected after Sue and Bob passed away. Seven years later, they asked their children to run the foundation, but to Sue and Bob's surprise, their children declined. The children weren't interested in rescuing dogs and cats; they were passionate about helping refugees from natural disasters . . . people misplaced by floods, famines, cyclones, etc.

Sue and Bob's "top-down" approach to keeping their kids connected through their foundation backfired because they didn't include their children in the decision process. No wonder the children balked. A "bottom-up" approach might have had their children craft the foundation's mission on their own, but that strategy would have failed too because Sue and Bob's passion was for animal rescues, not refugees. Although Sue and Bob's top-down approach was efficient and avoided conflict in the short term, asking their children to live with the consequences led to an unexpected, undesirable outcome.

Once the family recognized that they were trapped in a top-down :: bottom-up polarity, they used polarity thinking (described in chapter

9) to seek a both/and solution. They found one. After deeply exploring the motivation for each mission, the family realized that their shared passion was "homelessness," whether that meant refugees who lost their homes or pets looking for a loving home. They redrafted their foundation's mission to reflect this new understanding, and the children happily carried forth their parent's foundation for another generation.

Selective :: Inclusive

When Hamza married Zehra, Hamza challenged the historical decision that only bloodline family members participate in family council meetings. The policy was set when Hamza's older sister got married, but it made no sense to Hamza. He wanted his wife, the mother of their children, to learn about the history of the family business and participate in decisions made by the family council. "After all, these decisions affect her children too," said Hamza. "We need to be educated together if we're going to raise future owners of this family business," he reasoned.

Hamza's mother was dead set against it. She'd seen what could happen when married-ins who were raised with different values challenge long-standing beliefs in the family. "It gets messy," she said. "They see things differently than we do, and that slows us down. I don't care if Hamza thinks I'm overly controlling. I'm doing this for his protection."

Once Hamza and his mother recognized that they were stuck in a selective :: inclusive polarity, they used polarity thinking (described in chapter 9) to seek a both/and solution. They found one. Zehra would be invited to family council meetings and encouraged to participate in the discussions, but she would not have a vote. The voting control remained with the bloodline.

Structure :: Flexibility

The family employment policy was clear and strict: family members may apply for open positions in the family business only after they have five years of work experience outside of the family business and earned an MBA. The policy had served the business well for a decade.

Then Mathieu's son married Sylvie, a finance wizard who held a dual master's in accounting and economics, but not an MBA. As CEO, Mathieu needed to replace his retiring CFO and quickly recognized Sylvie's extensive talents, experience, and commitment to the family. How could he bypass the employment policy and hire Sylvie as CFO?

Once Mathieu recognized that he was stuck in a structure :: flexibility polarity, he used polarity thinking (described in chapter 9) to seek a both/and solution. He found one and brought it to the family council, whose mission had been to craft reliable family business policies. When he framed the opportunity to hire Sylvie as a structure :: flexibility polarity, the council issued an exception to the policy so Mathieu could offer the CFO position to Sylvie. She accepted.

Support :: Challenge

Julia and Julianna celebrated their son Bruno's university graduation in grand style, with a samba and funk band and a huge feast for family and friends. Bruno had completed his journalism degree with honors from the Universidade de São Paulo, and he was finally off the family books!

But Bruno struggled to find a job. The economy was in a downward cycle, and unemployment was growing. Nervously, he asked his moms if he could join the family business—a designer fashion department store chain with locations in São Paulo, Curitiba, and Florianópolis.

Julia and Julianna struggled with the decision. They didn't need journalists. They needed help managing the supply chain. Should they make up a job for him so he has an income? Julia was in favor—she couldn't bear the thought of her son struggling, and they were profitable enough to make up a job for him. Julianna, however, was against the idea. She thought it was important that her son struggle early in his career—overcoming challenges will make him a more resilient and mature professional.

Once Julie and Julianna recognized that they were stuck in a support :: challenge polarity, they used polarity thinking (described in chapter 9) to seek a both/and solution. They found one. They invited Bruno to move into their small, garage apartment, free of charge, while he looked for employment. The apartment wasn't fancy, and the air-conditioning was glitchy, but it provided him with the basics. Bruno was both grateful for the safe harbor and highly motivated to find a job where he could earn enough to upgrade his lifestyle.

Me :: We

From the beginning, Toskiki and Hanako crafted their hotel business for their eldest child, Akimi, who identifies as nonbinary and uses they/them pronouns. Known by their two siblings as "the smart one," Akimi was supposed to carry the business forward for the next generation. Akimi knew most aspects of operations thanks to numerous summer internships, and they were grateful that their parents were so generous and thoughtful in providing for Akimi's future.

But Akimi didn't like the hotel business. They toughed it out every summer because they knew it was what their parents wanted. Akimi had always been a dutiful child, eager to please their parents. But when it came down to having to choose whether to take over the business or do what their heart yearned to do, social work, Akimi felt torn between doing what was right for themself and doing what was right for the family.

Once Akimi recognized they were stuck in a me :: we polarity, they used polarity thinking (described in chapter 9) to seek a both/and solution. They found one. They found the courage to tell their parents that they didn't have an interest in the hotel business. Their sister Masaki, however, loved the hotel business. She'd worked there every summer as well, so they recommended that Masaki take over leadership of the business, and Akimi offered to serve on the family business board.

That gave them an opportunity to both support the family business at a strategic level and follow their passion as a social worker.

The Blind Men and an Elephant

Because family businesses are complex systems encompassing multiple perspectives, the parable of the blind men and an elephant is an apt metaphor describing the value of family business governance. Six blind men encounter an elephant for the first time, and each describes the elephant based on what he feels:

- The first man touches the trunk and claims the elephant is like a thick snake.
- The next man touches the ear and claims the elephant is like a fan.
- Another man touches a leg and claims an elephant is like the trunk of a tree.
- The next man feels its tusk and claims an elephant is like a spear.
- Another feels the animal's side and claims an elephant is like a wall.
- The last man feels the tail and claims an elephant is like a rope.

Eventually, each of the six blind men concludes that the others are dishonest, and they come to blows. The moral of the story is that we tend to believe an absolute truth based on our subjective experiences, ignoring other people's subjective yet equally true ones.

This concept is easily extended to a family business system. John Davis and Renato Tagiuri developed the *three-circle model*[78] in the 1970s to help the interdependent stakeholders in a family business—the family, the owners, and the employees—get on the balcony to see the entire (figurative) elephant. The framework below graphically depicts the seven different interest groups, "each with its own legitimate perspectives, goals and dynamics."

---

78 John A. Davis, accessed March 3, 2024, https://johndavis.com/three-circle-model-family-business-system.

Three-Circle Model
of the Family Business System

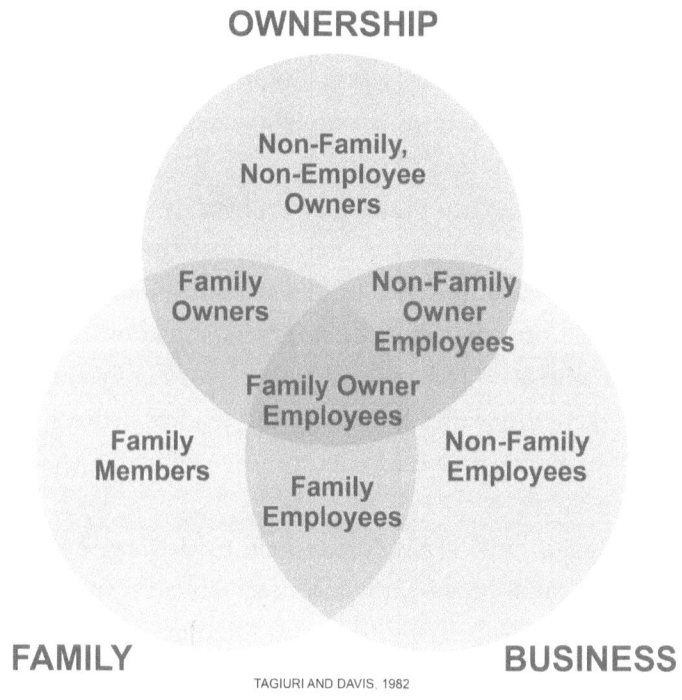

TAGIURI AND DAVIS, 1982

Each circle represents a separate collection of interests:
- Family interests include harmony, unity, acceptance, loyalty;
- Business interests include profitability, market share, innovation, growth; and
- Ownership interests include return on investment, stock appreciation, dividend distributions, voting control.

In addition, each circle can overlap with another circle, resulting in seven different possible perspectives, each distinct from the others. These different perspectives, when viewed from that perspective alone, lead to conflict just like the blind men describing the elephant. Each perspective is valid and true, and not everyone can see the system from a perspective other than their own. The lack of a "system" perspective leads to judgments of others such as stingy, grandiose, lazy, selfish, naïve, stupid, foolhardy, etc.

For example, when a family member's perspective is "family owner," then his interests are typically focused on the business's dividends. He may not have visibility into the investment needs of the business—the business is simply a resource for distributions, a goose that lays some golden eggs.

In contrast, when a family member's perspective is "family employee," then her priority may be investing in the business. Because she prefers to invest profits in the business to create more value in the future, she's often labeled "stingy" and/or "selfish." It's the family member who is *both* family owner *and* family employee who is more likely to intuitively manage the tension between dividends and reinvestment because she can feel the competing commitments within herself.

The Tagiuri and Davis "three-circle model" helps ease conflict in family business because it enables each "blind man" touching the "elephant" to empathize with the other blind men's perspectives.

To learn more about in family business governance, read Josh Baron and Rob Lachenauer's book the *Harvard Business Review Family Business Handbook: How to Build and Sustain a Successful, Enduring Enterprise* originally published in 2021.

I hope these examples have whet your appetite for the next chapter—the most important chapter of the book—"Embracing Polarities to Harmonize Opposites." At last, chapters 9 and 10 describe *how* to navigate the countless polarities mentioned throughout the book.

Questions for Chapter 8

1. How will you know when your family business is ready to introduce (or update) more formal family governance? Hint: are the right people making the right decisions at the right time?
2. How well are you managing these four polarities: top down :: bottom up, selective :: inclusive, support :: challenge, and structure :: flexibility?
3. Where do you reside in the three-circle model? How does that position shape your perspective of the family business?
4. If you are in conflict with someone in the family business, where do they reside in the three-circle model? How might that shape their perspective of the family business?

"How wonderful that we have met with a paradox. Now we have some hope of making progress."

—NIELS BOHR

CHAPTER 9
EMBRACING POLARITIES TO HARMONIZE OPPOSITES

By now, I hope you have seen yourself in one or more of the stories and even absorbed some of the fundamentals about polarities: that they are interdependent pairs of equally important yet seemingly opposing values, that either side of the polarity by itself becomes problematic, and that much conflict in family businesses is born from trying to "solve" a polarity by choosing one of the values as "the solution." Polarities are not solvable. Polarities need to be managed over time. This chapter is all about how.

I have winnowed the complex topic of polarities into ten fundamental principles described below. Take your time reading this chapter because it's dense, and the concept of polarities takes time to fully grasp. Once you understand them, however, you may begin to see polarities *everywhere*. I am convinced that leveraging polarities is a leadership superpower, one that's remarkably important in family business leadership.

10 Polarity Principles:

1. Polarities can't be solved; they must be managed.
2. Both pole values in a polarity tension are necessary, over time. Neither pole alone is sufficient to create and sustain high performance.
3. An overfocus on one pole while neglecting the other will guarantee the overuse of the preferred pole.
4. When we experience the overuse of one pole, we (tend to) see the benefits of the other pole as a "solution," so we swing to that other pole and expose ourselves to its overuses.
5. We all have pole preferences. Our preferences are born from an aversion to the *overuse* of the opposite pole.
6. "Arguing the diagonals" puts one force against the other because both poles are "right." Each diagonal point of view is correct but, on its own, incomplete.
7. To leverage the ongoing tension in any polarity, supplement either/or thinking with both/and thinking.[79]
8. Strong pole preferences are frequently connected to a strength and/or identity.
9. Harmonizing poles (both/and thinking) may necessitate facing your fears.
10. The greater the desire for the benefits of one pole, the greater the tolerance for its overuse because these overuses are considered "less bad" than the overuses of the other pole.

---

79   . . . for those tensions that require both/and thinking. Sometimes, we accept one pole with intention.

Polarity Principle #1: Polarities can't be solved; they must be managed.

Unavoidable and indestructible, polarities are interdependent pairs, like inhaling and exhaling. In continuous tension, they define each other. Without one, the other doesn't exist. Although they appear to be opposing, they are, instead, mutually supportive.

Every pole in a polarity has benefits and overuse risks. The "overuses" are the outcomes of overvaluing one pole value to the neglect of the other. To see how a polarity works, map its predictable dynamic. Although the graphic may look like a simple two-by-two matrix, there's an important difference. Mapping the polarity helps you appreciate how each part relates to the other parts in the matrix.

The top of the matrix defines the why—the aspiration for managing this polarity well. The bottom of the matrix defines the aversion—that which you seek to avoid. As an example, here's an inhale :: exhale polarity map that exemplifies the interdependent pair concept as well as introduces the benefits and overuses of each pole:

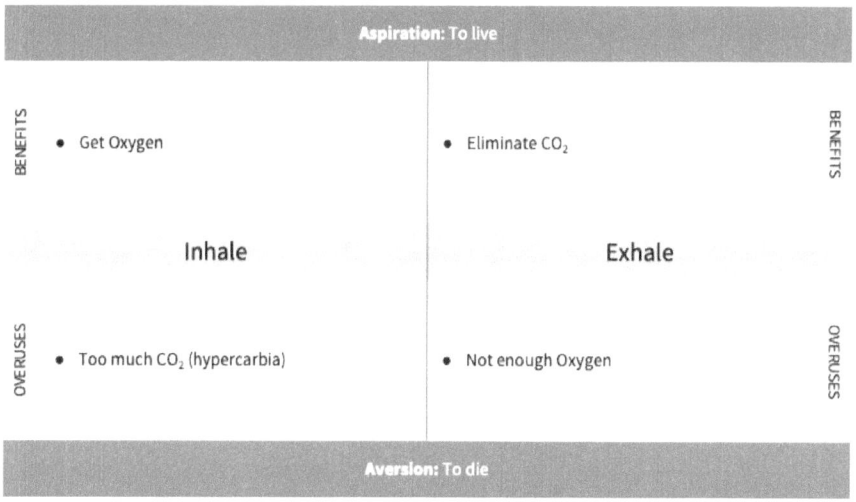

The benefit of inhaling is getting oxygen. The overuse of inhaling (inhaling without exhaling) is hypercarbia—too much carbon dioxide in our bodies. The benefit of exhaling is eliminating the carbon dioxide. The overuse of exhaling (exhaling without inhaling) is a lack of oxygen. See how these quadrants are interconnected?

Our bodies manage the tension between inhaling and exhaling in a somewhat rhythmic fashion: we inhale until we no longer need oxygen; then we exhale to expel carbon dioxide until we're ready for more oxygen, so we inhale, etc. We stay alive by managing this inhale :: exhale polarity for the rest of our lives.

With a family business, this same ongoing tension exists. Much like *both* inhaling *and* exhaling is needed to live, *both* the family *and* the business is needed to be a family business. It's not a polarity in nature like wet :: dry—you can have a family without a business, and you can have a business without a family—but if you have a family business, you are managing a family :: business polarity. Thankfully, "managing the polarity" is how you make decisions and climb your way out of conflict and indecision.

Polarity Principle #2: Both pole values in a polarity tension are necessary, over time. Neither pole alone is sufficient to create and sustain high performance.

Nobody asks whether you should inhale or exhale to live. You wouldn't survive long if you inhaled without exhaling, or vice versa. In a family business, the same is true for the family and business polarity. Seeing family and business as a polarity helps you appreciate how to achieve a thriving family and business. This is why adopting a "family-first" or "business-first" policy can be problematic and lead to breaking up the family or destroying the business.

Not convinced? Let's map the family-first :: business-first polarity:

	Aspiration: Thriving family and business	
BENEFITS	• We ensure the financial needs of family members are considered and addressed. • We work through relationship conflict so it doesn't fester. • We conduct performance reviews with family to support continual development. • We enjoy the privileges of ownership.	• We ensure the business is profitable and healthy. • We vigorously debate the best ideas. • We challenge family members to be their best and hold them accountable. • We responsibly allocate profits for both reinvestment and ownership dividends.
	Family-First	**Business-First**
OVERUSES	• We overpay family members. • We avoid conflict to preserve family harmony. • We exclude family from performance reviews to avoid hurting their feelings. • We overconsume business profits and underinvest in the business.	• We underpay family to invest in the business. • We engage in constant, destructive conflict. • We hold family members to impossible standards. • We issue no/low dividends, leaving some owners questioning the value of ownership.
	Aversion: Ailing family and/or business	

A singular focus on family-first can lead to problems for the business, and a singular focus on business-first can lead to problems for the family. Family business leaders must consider *both* the needs of the family *and* the needs of the business for long-term sustainability. Asking whether a family business should be a family-first business or a business-first business is like asking whether one should inhale or exhale to stay alive. It's the wrong question. The right question is "How do we navigate the inherent tension that exists between the family and the business so that we get the best for both the family and the business?"

Polarity Principle #3: An overfocus on one pole while neglecting the other will guarantee the overuse of the preferred pole.

For this principle, let's explore the tension between the management styles of support :: challenge first introduced in chapter 3. For context, let's assume your aspiration is a rising generation of employees who thrive with confidence in the workplace. To see a more complete picture of the tension, we map the polarity:

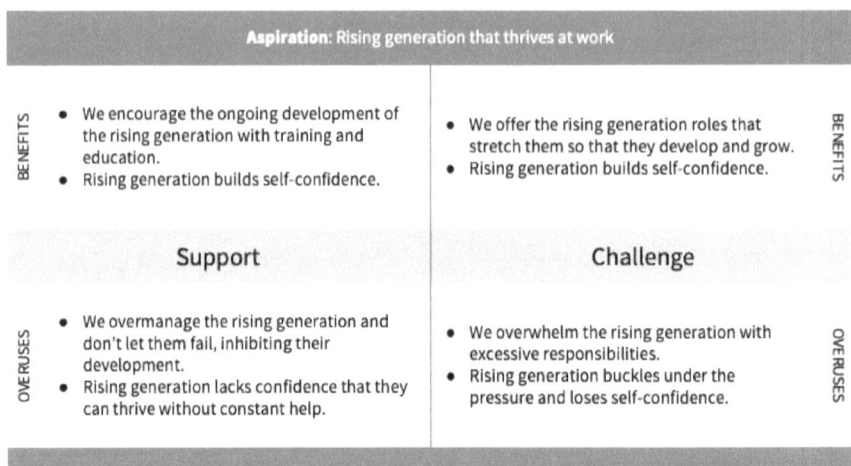

What happens if you provide the rising generation with only support and no challenge? Or all challenge and no support?

According to this polarity principle, when you only support employees, you're guaranteed to experience its overuses. As an example, let's extend this support :: challenge polarity to parenting styles: excessive support (helicoptering) prevents children from failing, but *people learn from failure*. When you teach your kids how to ride a bike, you don't hold on to the back of the bike forever. You run beside them for a while, then let go. Of course, they fall, it hurts, and then they get back on the bike. That's how they learn and grow confidence. They triumph in the face of adversity.

Why should that change when they're adults in the workplace? If you never metaphorically let go of the back of their bikes, the rising generation won't gain confidence that they can do it on their own. Instead, they'll become dependent on you. Goethe described it succinctly over 200 years ago: "Too many parents make life hard for their children by trying, too zealously, to make it easy for them."

Conversely, when you only challenge employees, you're guaranteed to experience its overuses. You may overwhelm them and thwart their ability to earn some wins, thus undermining their self-confidence. You also run the risk of driving them out of the business because they're not getting much enjoyment at work. Constant failure just isn't fun.

Developmental psychologist and Harvard professor Robert Kegan describes the need for both support and challenge: "... people grow best where they continuously experience an ingenious blend of support and challenge; the rest is commentary. Environments that are weighted too heavily in the direction of challenge without adequate support are toxic; they promote defensiveness and constriction. Those weighted too heavily toward support without adequate challenge are ultimately boring; they promote devitalization."[80]

PRO TIP

A note about mapping polarities. Strive for an equal number of benefits and overuses in each quadrant. If you can't find an equal number, you may have a blind spot. Polarities have an energy like an infinity loop cycling through the four quadrants.

Let's examine a common leadership polarity such as task :: relationship. Assume I prefer to focus on tasks because I believe in efficiency . . . and relationships take too much time. On the upside, I accomplish much. Bing, bang, boom. However, I soon realize that my team is growing resentful because I'm not involving them in decisions. As I experience the overuse of tasks, I swing to focus on relationships to build consensus, but soon, I get anxious because it takes time to bring others along. Then, I swing back to focusing on the task, and the energy cycle repeats.

BOTTOM LINE: IF YOU HAVE AN IMBALANCE IN YOUR POLARITY MAP, IDENTIFY THE ENERGY CYCLE(S) FOR EACH POLARITY.

---

80 Robert Kegan, *In Over Our Heads: The Mental Demands of Modern Life*, (Cambridge: Harvard University Press, 1994), 42.

Polarity Principle #4: When we experience the overuses of one pole, we (tend to) see the benefits of the other pole as a "solution," so we swing to that other pole and expose ourselves to its overuses.

We see this in large organizations that famously swing between centralized and decentralized decision-making[81]: Imagine a new CEO hears complaint after complaint from the field locations that headquarters can't make decisions fast enough. Worse, the blanket decisions from HDQ don't meet the unique needs of each field office. So, she heroically decentralizes decision-making by authorizing each field location to make its own rules. This works beautifully at first, but six years later, the CEO is ousted because the corporate brand has been diluted and the field offices are running amok. Enter the new CEO, who hears the complaints and heroically centralizes the decision authority back to HDQ, and the cycle continues.

Applied to family business, this polarity seesaw tends to show up in family businesses succession as described by Amy Schuman, Stacy Stutz, and John Ward in their book, *Family Business as Paradox*.[82] They describe three common swings in leadership style between the first and second generations:

- Action :: Planning—founding generations (G1) tend to favor action and opportunism over reflection and strategy. G2, after witnessing the overuse of unplanned action, tends to favor reflection and planning.
- Expedience :: Process—G1 tends to lean toward the pragmatic and practical, while G2 tends to prefer organization and structure.

---

81 Andrew Campbell, Sven Kunisch, and Günter Müller-Stewens, "To centralize or not to centralize?" *McKinsey & Company*, June 1, 2011, accessed March 4, 2024, https://www.mckinsey.com/capabilities/people-and-organizational-performance/our-insights/to-centralize-or-not-to-centralize.

82 This terrific book offers a deep analysis of many more polarities in family business. I particularly appreciate their intergenerational analysis in chapter 3 and the predictable tensions that arise in the intersections of the three circles in the 3-Circle Model by Tagiuri and Davis: family, ownership, and business in chapter 4. Amy Schuman, Stacy Stutz, and John L. Ward, *Family Business as Paradox*, (New York: Palgrave MacMillan, 2010.)

- Directive :: Participative—G1 is accustomed to directing and controlling outcomes. G2 siblings, who make decisions as a group, lean toward participative or collective decision-making.

According to the authors, the third generation in a family business tends to manage these tensions better than G1 and G2 because they have witnessed the overuse of both extremes in prior generations. They naturally seek the benefits of both poles through the integration of opposites.

Polarity Principle #5: We all have pole preferences. Our preferences are born from an aversion to the *overuse* of the opposite pole.

For this principle, let's explore the reveal :: conceal polarity introduced in chapter 1 and common in estate planning and family offices. A frequent sticking point with families with significant wealth, the reveal :: conceal tension arises when communicating the scope of the family's wealth to one's descendants. The leading generation famously struggles with the question, *should we reveal our estate to our children, or should we conceal it?* In that context, let's map the polarity:

	Aspiration: Descendants prepared for a healthy future	
BENEFITS	• The rising generation can conduct personal financial planning with reliable information. • The rising generation builds skills to prepare for the responsibilities of wealth. • We invite the rising generation to influence estate plans because they will live with the outcomes.	• The rising generation develops healthy self-esteem, purpose, and skills. • The rising generation is unburdened by the responsibilities of inherited wealth. • The leading generation doesn't have to defend their decisions to rising generation.
	Reveal	**Conceal**
OVERUSES	• The rising generation fails to develop healthy self-esteem and lives an entitled lifestyle. • The rising generation feels overwhelmed with the responsibilities of inherited wealth. • The leading generation has to defend their decisions with the rising generation.	• The rising generation spends a career doing work they loathe, missing the opportunity to pursue their passions. • The rising generation is unprepared for the responsibilities of wealth. • The needs of the rising generation are not considered.
	Aversion: Descendants' lives constrained by inheritance	

Not only do individual family members prefer one pole over the other, but so do most family business advisers (and they may not realize it). Parents who favor reveal are likely to have a strong aversion to an overuse of conceal. They might fear that their children will unnecessarily earn a living doing work that they hate. In contrast, parents who favor conceal are likely to have a strong aversion to the overuse of reveal, such as having to defend their estate planning decisions with their children.

PRO TIP

Make sure the names of each pole in the polarity use neutral or positive terms. For example, the interdependent pair of conceal is not entitled. Entitled is an overuse of reveal. Reveal is a more neutral term to pair with conceal. Similarly, assume you recognize that "activity" is one pole of a polarity, and you want to choose a term that represents the other pole. Lazy? Nope—that's an overuse risk of the other pole. A neutral or positive term might be "rest," so the polarity can be activity :: rest.

Polarity Principle #6: "Arguing the diagonals" puts one force against the other because both poles are "right." Each diagonal point of view is correct but, on its own, incomplete.

For this principle, let's map the invest :: harvest polarity introduced in chapter 1. This is the polarity in which many families get stuck when deciding how to allocate profits in a family business.

	Aspiration: Thriving family and business	
BENEFITS	• Our investment in infrastructure and brand relevance keeps us thriving. • We leverage "patient" capital by investing in long-term bets with high ROIs. • We don't raise entitled heirs.	• We use profits to diversify away from a single asset or industry. • We issue dividends to enhance owners' lifestyles. • Non-operating owners feel value from and connected to the family business.	**BENEFITS**
	Invest	**Harvest**	
OVERUSES	• We are overexposed to a single asset or industry due to lack of diversification. • Profit reinvestments inhibit the ability to enhance family member lifestyles. • Non-operating owners feel disconnected and/or resentful of the business due to low dividends.	• We have outdated infrastructure and/or lack marketplace relevance due to underinvestment. • We diversify investment into assets with poor returns. • We limit the incentive to work due to excess dividends.	**OVERUSES**
	Aversion: Ailing family and/or business	

Typically, operating owners favor the invest strategy, nonoperating owners favor the harvest strategy, and each side argues its point of view as the diagonal on the polarity map. The operating owners argue the benefits of investing and the overuses of harvesting, whereas the nonoperating owners argue the benefits of harvesting and the overuses of investing.

"Arguing the diagonals[83]" places force against force, with no winner because *both are right*. Investing in the business is right; harvesting from the business is right. This is why leaders must reframe these challenges from problems (an either/or question with no right answer) to polarities (a both/and question with answers that dynamically change over time).

As you read this, ask yourself, *Which pole do I prefer? Invest or harvest?* Now, if you are a part of a family business, locate yourself in the "three-circle model"[84], introduced in chapter 8:

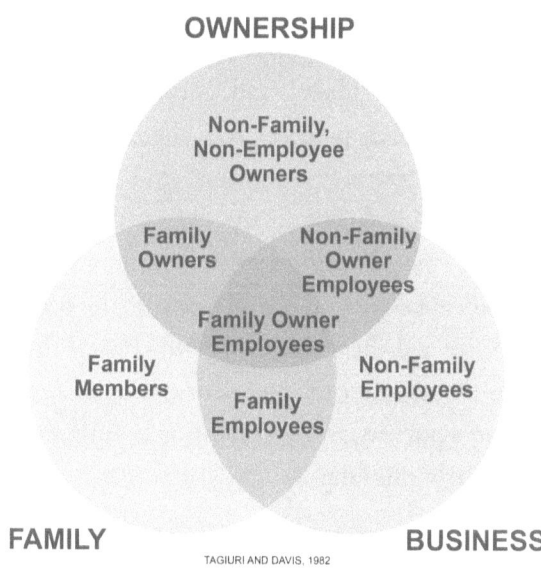

---

83 The concept of 'arguing the diagonals' comes from Brian Emerson and Kelly Lewis's book *Navigating Polarities: Using Both/And Thinking to Lead Transformation*, (Washington: Paradoxical Press, 2019).
84 John A. Davis, accessed March 3, 2024, https://johndavis.com/three-circle-model-family-business-system.

How does your location in the "three-circle model" influence your pole preference? How might the placement of other members of the family business influence their pole preferences? Assume you identify as a "family owner." It's likely you would argue in favor of harvesting profits through dividends to owners. In the absence of dividends or employment, owning a large, illiquid asset provides little tangible value. To the contrary, it carries the responsibility of stewarding the asset for future generations.

Next, assume you identify with the "family employee" section of the model above. From this perspective, you'd be more likely to argue in favor of investing profits back into the business. Maybe you'd like to fund an R&D project or launch a new marketing campaign—a near-term investment that will grow the long-term value of the business.

PRO TIP

Family business polarities aren't the only polarities families fight about. Politics, for example, can be extremely polarizing in families. Consider liberal and conservative ideologies as a polarity.[85] With which pole do you align? Map out your own polarity map for liberal :: conservative. Knowing the benefits of your preferred ideology and the overuses of the other should come easily to you. Challenge yourself to name the overuses of your preferred ideology and the benefits of the other. Imagine a world where we had the benefits of both conservative and liberal ideology. In theory, we can, once our politicians recognize they are trapped in a polarity and switch from arguing the diagonals to both/and polarity thinking.

The question "should we invest or harvest" is *the wrong question* because it uses either/or thinking when both/and is needed. It doesn't

---

[85] Jonathan Haidt, "The moral roots of liberals and conservatives," *TED*, March 2008, accessed March 3, 2024, https://www.ted.com/talks/jonathan_haidt_the_moral_roots_of_liberals_and_conservatives.

capture the complexity of the decision and misses out on strategies that create greater value for all involved. When managing a polarity, the questions need to change. Better questions might be, "When and how much should we invest? When and how much should we harvest?" The better answer is one that meets the unique needs of the family and the business at a specific point in time. That answer may change over time, as the family changes, as the business changes, and as the business climate changes.

For example, in one year, the profits might be split 80 percent for the business to pay for a copyright infringement lawsuit and 20 percent to owners. In the next year, the profits might be split 25 percent to the business and 75 percent to the owners to finance a down payment on a retirement home. For some families, a win-win is reinvesting 100 percent of the profits back into the business. For others, it could be a third to the business, a third to owners, and a third to build a cash reserve for any family member who wants to be bought out of their ownership. It all depends on the needs of the business and the needs of the owners. The key is to seek strategies that accrue the benefits of *both* investing *and* harvesting.

In a related example, imagine a family council crafts a clear distribution policy. For most years, this policy will serve the family and business just fine. And in other years, the policy may be too rigid to take advantage of unique business or family conditions. Here we have a structure :: flexibility polarity. The policy offers the benefits of structure, but in certain years, the structure becomes a problem—it's too rigid, and the family needs flexibility. See how polarities can be layered and complex? The process of mapping polarities supports the dynamic decision-making family business leaders need.

Last, in one final "arguing the diagonals" example, I frequently see family members completely miss each other when communicating. One argues with feelings (family mindset) and the other argues with reason (business mindset). They simply can't hear each other because their brains are wired for the opposite of what they hear, so they spin their wheels arguing the diagonals over and over and over again. The beauty of polarity thinking is that it enables you lead with *both* love *and* logic.

Polarity Principle #7: To leverage the ongoing tension in any polarity, supplement either/or thinking with both/and thinking.[86]

In the 1970s, Dr. Barry Johnson[87] put polarities on the map when he developed a framework to manage the tension in any polarity. Polarity Thinking replaces either/or decisions with both/and ones and is a leadership superpower for leveraging the tension in these unsolvable problems. It invites us to think creatively about how to capture the benefits of *both* poles and mitigate the overuse risks of either one.

Polarity management is particularly useful in family businesses when multiple family members prefer opposing poles. The Polarity Map can be used to help each "faction" appreciate the benefits of their non-preferred pole and understand the overuse risks of their preferred pole. By appreciating the predictable way polarities work, conversations shift from "I'm right and you're wrong" to "Ah, I see we want the same things—we want to reap the benefits of both poles." We stop arguing over "this *or* that" and start asking, "How can we get both of this *and* that?" Best of all, polarity thinking shifts the conversation *away* from defending your positions and *toward* advocating for your interests, which fosters creativity in crafting solutions.

Managing polarities isn't about trade-offs or compromise. It is simply using the right tool for the job so you creatively accrue the best of both and avoid the problems of either. Much like inhaling and

---

86 Sometimes we tolerate one pole with conscious intention.
87 Barry Johnson, *Polarity Management: Identifying and Managing Unsolvable Problems*, (Amherst: HRD Press), 1992. Barry Johnson, *And: Making a Difference by Leveraging Polarity, Paradox or Dilemma, Volume One.* (Amherst: HRD Press), 2020. Barry Johnson, *And: Making a Difference by Leveraging Polarity, Paradox or Dilemma, Volume Two* (Amherst: HRD Press), 2021. Learn more at www.polaritypartnerships.com and www.polarityresources.com.

exhaling to live, you don't compromise by hovering in the middle.

Let's ground this theory in some family business practice.[88] One common polarity families face, especially during periods of leadership and ownership succession, is the tension between tradition and innovation, which we first explored in chapter 7. Typically, the leading generation values tradition, and the rising generation values innovation. Let's look at some frequent benefits and overuses of each pole:

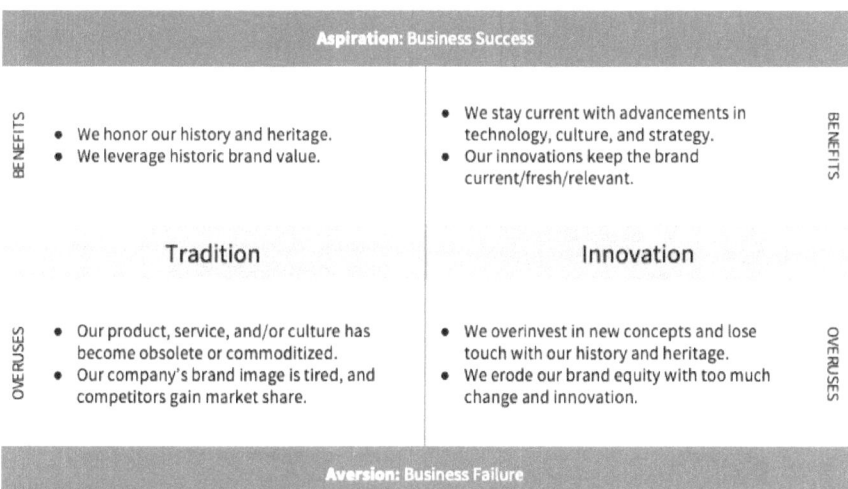

Families who get stuck in an ongoing battle for whether to maintain tradition *or* innovate can use this framework to explore the benefits of both tradition *and* innovation. Once they have developed their Polarity Map, they can identify which overuses they are experiencing currently, which benefits they are missing out on, and whether they are overvaluing one pole to the neglect of the other. Then, the family can stop arguing about the diagonals and start to develop strategies that capture the benefits of each pole.

Remember, because there's no "best answer" with polarities—only better answers—each family will integrate the family mindset and business mindset differently. For one family, that might mean going

---

88 Note, theory :: practice is itself a polarity!

all in on innovation and investing 100 percent of the profits into AI. For another family, it might mean investing 20 percent in AI and 80 percent in a fresh ad campaign to ensure the traditional product lines don't get stale.

Polarity Principle #8: Strong pole preferences are frequently connected to a strength and/or identity.

For this principle, I'm choosing a polarity that I struggle with personally—responsibility :: privilege (first introduced in chapter 5). Not all polarities are connected to one's identity, but the responsibility :: privileges polarity sure can be. Here's a possible polarity map for this tension:

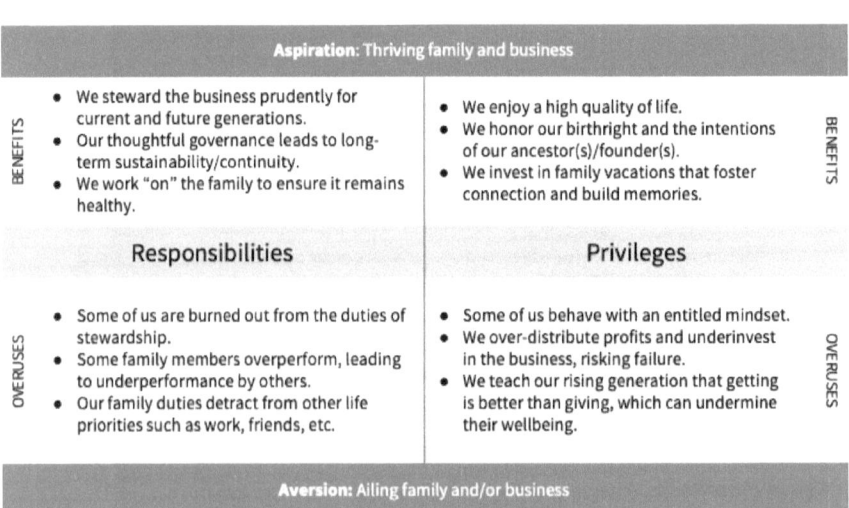

Modern media[89] loves to portray members of family businesses (especially heirs) as entitled brats who abuse their privilege by spending lavishly on themselves without consideration of others. Yes, some family business members *do* exhibit entitled behaviors, but in my experience, most family business members don't. Much of chapter 5 describes the anguish of responsibility, not privilege. The emotional pain of working in a family business is real and hard, and family

---
89 HBO's *Succession* is a great example in the 2020s. *Dallas* is a great example in the 1980s.

business leaders I know tend to favor responsibility over privilege.

I, too, favor the responsibility pole. It wasn't until I forced myself to map the responsibility :: privileges polarity that I realized I had a large blind spot related to responsibility. I unconsciously clung to responsibility in fiery rejection of the overuses of privileges, but I couldn't see how deeply I lived in the overuse of responsibility.

In their book *Navigating Polarities*, authors Emerson and Lewis developed a "key" to help people "deepen their awareness and acceptance of their relationship" to a polarity.[90] I've simplified their brilliant key below into what I call an identity x-ray, which decodes your self-image in any identity-related polarity. Here's how it works:

IDENTITY X-RAY

BENEFITS	Preferred Pole	Non-preferred Pole	BENEFITS
	• How I want to be seen • What I want to be known for	• Missing qualities that inhibit my effectiveness • Untapped skills	
OVERUSES	• How others might view me • Blind spots	• Things I don't want to be associated with or known for • Things I dislike in other people	OVERUSES

- *The benefits of our preferred pole are what we want to be known for and how we want to be seen.* Oh, how I want to be known for being a responsible steward. I want my long-dead grandfather (the G1 in our family) to feel proud that his granddaughter is stewarding his assets responsibly on behalf of his future descendants. I take pride in living well within my means and sharing my prosperity with others who weren't born with this

---

90   Brian Emerson and Kelly Lewis, *Navigating Polarities: Using Both/And Thinking to Lead Transformation*, (Washington: Paradoxical Press, 2019), 143.

same advantage. To me, that feels like the responsible thing to do, and I want to be seen as "responsible."

- *The overuses of our preferred pole are how others might view us and reveal potential blind spots.* However, my attachment to responsibility drives me to overperform. People often asked me why I push myself so hard, why I don't take many vacations, and why I let myself get so tense, tired, and overworked. To be honest, I work hard to earn the advantage that I was born into; I do it to assuage my false guilt.
- *The benefits of our non-preferred pole are missing qualities that inhibit our effectiveness and possible untapped skills.* Yes, by overfocusing on responsibilities, I bury my head in work and miss opportunities to connect with friends or have fun. This undermines my fundamental well-being. In addition, my refusal to rely on a penny of inherited money almost held me back from becoming a leadership coach. I didn't know how long it would take for me to become self-sustainable as a coach, and I scorned the idea of dipping into inherited assets to live. In retrospect, I'm glad I took the risk because being a leadership coach for family business leaders is possibly the best way I can be of value to the world. Well, that, and writing this book!
- *The overuses of my non-preferred pole are things we don't want to be known for and things we don't like in others.* For a long time, I felt shame for being born into the lucky sperm club. I didn't earn this advantage. It was given to me. I absolutely didn't want to be known for being an entitled brat. The social message I absorbed was "rich kids are bad people," and I didn't want people to think I was bad. As for disliking this behavior in others? Well, my father exhibited behavior that was far closer to the privileges pole than the responsibility pole, and if you recall my story in the introduction, it may not surprise you that I formed an identity at a young age of "I'm not like him."

The polarities that are related to identity are the hardest to acknowledge, address, and reconcile because they necessitate facing fears.

Polarity Principle #9: Harmonizing poles (both/and thinking) may necessitate facing your fears.

Once I realized I was overfocused on responsibility, I had to identify the benefits and face my identity fears related to privilege. Both challenged me. It took a long time for me to acknowledge the benefits of privilege. This isn't a humble brag. I recognize how ridiculous it sounds. As a child, my shame in being born into a family of means was so strong that I wouldn't touch my privilege so I could fit in with friends who didn't have it. My elders warned me not to get too big for my britches, that I put my pants on one leg at a time just like everyone else, that if I reveal any privilege, I could get kidnapped and held for ransom. I was terrified to acknowledge privilege! It made me feel vulnerable and shameful.

Strangely, I had buried these beliefs and held them to be true for so many decades that all of this shame remained unconscious until I learned about polarities and mapped my own responsibility :: privileges polarity map. Since then, I've been facing the discomfort of enjoying privileges (even spending the savings I've earned on my own!), conducting my own safe-to-fail experiments, and reading many of shame-researcher Brené Brown's books. Thankfully, this work has helped me have a more peaceful relationship with this polarity tension—and with myself.

Applying this to family business, let's imagine Wes, a talented, early-forties COO, is pawing at the ground to succeed his mother as CEO. In deciding how to approach her, he realizes that he is facing a cooperate :: confront polarity.

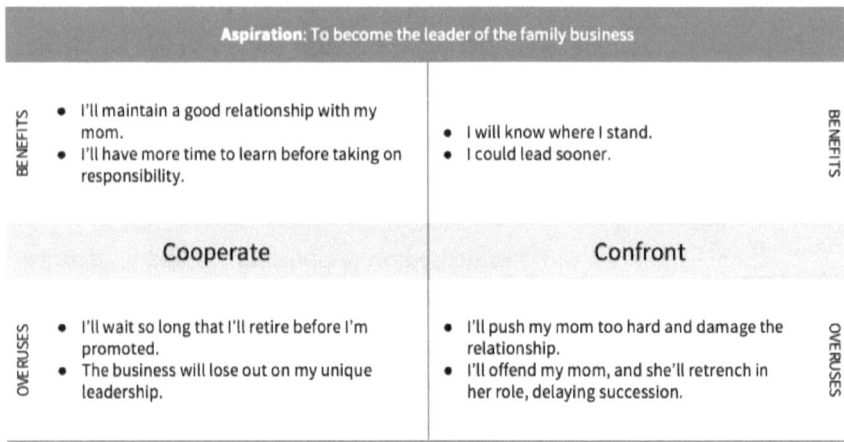

Because Wes had studied polarity thinking, he knew to explore how to get the benefits of *both* confronting *and* cooperating instead of choosing one or the other. However, both/and thinking left him uncomfortable because he had a huge aversion to confrontation. His mother didn't take well to it. He vividly remembered when he confronted her about extending his freedoms as a teenager. . . . Instead of extending his curfew, she *tightened* it, and he didn't want to play with fire on this issue with stakes so high.

For Wes, harmonizing poles[91] required facing his fears because the stronger the aversion to one pole (in his case, confront), the more vulnerable it feels to use it. It also required him to develop new skills because he wasn't practiced at confronting his mother. At the start of chapter 10, we'll revisit Wes's story to learn how he planned his next moves.

PRO TIP

I have listed many common polarities related to leadership, family businesses, governance, succession, and estate planning at

---

91 Brian Emerson and Kelly Lewis, *Navigating Polarities: Using Both/And Thinking to Lead Transformation*, (Washington: Paradoxical Press, 2019).

the end of this chapter so you can explore your own blind spots and opportunities for development. I recommend the book *Navigating Polarities* by Brian Emerson and Kelly Lewis to dive deeper into understanding and harmonizing polarities.[92] Even the Myers-Briggs MBTI assessment,[93] one of the oldest personality assessments in human history, is a set of four polarities: extraversion :: introversion, sensing :: intuition, thinking :: feeling, and judging :: perceiving.

Polarity Principle #10: The greater the desire for the benefits of one pole, the greater the tolerance of its overuses because these overuses are considered "less bad" than the overuses of the other pole.

For this principle, let's unpack the exclude :: include polarity in the context of whether to invite married-ins to work in the family business—a common sticking point in crafting a family employment policy. Here's a sample polarity map for the exclude :: include polarity:

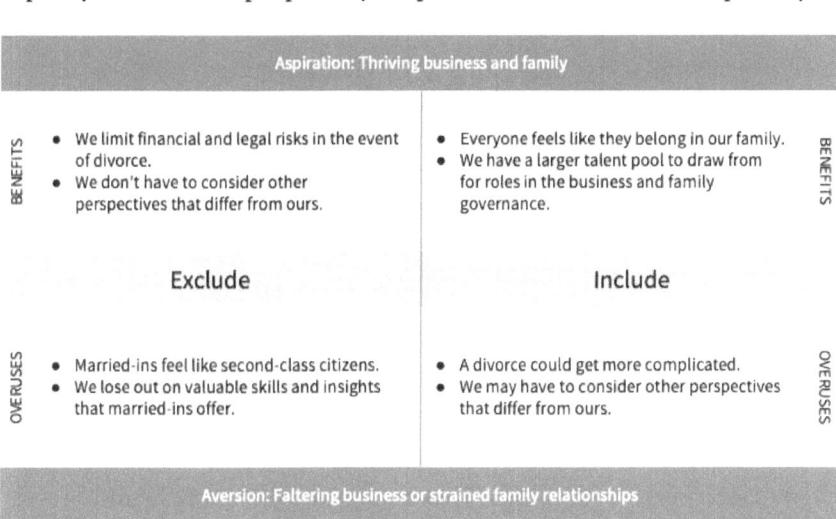

---

92 Brian Emerson and Kelly Lewis, *Navigating Polarities: Using Both/And Thinking to Lead Transformation*, (Washington: Paradoxical Press, 2019).
93 The Myers-Briggs Company, "Myers-Briggs Type Indicator® (MBTI®)," accessed March 3, 2024, https://www.themyersbriggs.com/en-US/Products-and-Services/Myers-Briggs.

Principle #10 says that the greater the conviction to exclude married-ins from working in the company, the greater the tolerance of the overuses of exclusion—creating the feeling of second-class citizens and/or missing out on their valuable skills. Conversely, the greater the attachment to including married-ins on the payroll, the greater the tolerance of possible poor performance and/or complications from unwinding a professional relationship in the event of divorce.

Without framing this as a polarity, families get stuck arguing for an all-or-nothing, either/or policy. Per Polarity Principle #6, "arguing the diagonals" just puts force against force with no way out. Recognizing this as a polarity shifts the either/or argument to a collective brainstorm that gets the benefits of both poles. What would it take for everyone to feel like they belong, you limit financial and legal risks in the event of divorce, you have a larger talent pool to choose from, and you don't have to consider other perspectives that differ from the norms of your family of origin? There are lots of creative ways to achieve those outcomes. Plus, you may still choose an all-or-nothing policy, but at least you won't be surprised when the overuses arise.

Managing polarities isn't easy for the weak of heart. It requires that we hold the tension of opposites to be both true. It means tolerating the ambiguity of not having a clear "right answer" and accepting that these tensions cannot be solved; they can only be managed. Those who can hold the discomfort of paradox are truly the most transformational leaders among us. In the absence of polarity awareness, we tend to drive harder with the strategies we believe to be right, and our problem-solving mentality simply exacerbates the problem. Polarity thinking gives us access to fresh strategies, novel thought processes, and new possibilities.

In chapter 10, you will learn a four-step process that develops strategies to manage these dilemmas using familiar family business scenarios.

Questions for Chapter 9

1. What recurring arguments are you having that have you stuck, putting force against force with no solution? Might you be arguing the diagonals of a polarity? If yes, map the polarity and change the conversation to harmonize the poles. (Hint: spend :: save is a common polarity in marriages!)
2. At the end of this chapter, I've listed some common polarities. Choose a polarity from the "leadership" list for which you have a strong pole preference and map the polarity with your preferred pole on the left. Then check it against the identity x-ray from Polarity Principle #8. What blind spots are revealed? What skills can you develop?
3. Bonus: If you follow US politics, challenge yourself to map the liberal :: conservative polarity (and place your preferred pole on the left side of the map). What do you notice?

    a. What does the identity x-ray in Polarity Principle #8 reveal to you?

    b. Which US states might be experiencing an overuse of liberal? Which US states might be experiencing an overuse of conservative?

    c. What benefits would both/and policies offer?

    d. What fears would a both/and strategy force you to face?

    e. On what issues are US politicians the most stuck, and how might they be arguing the diagonals?

Common Leadership Polarities

- My way :: your way
- Control :: trust
- Doing :: delegating
- Relaxed :: driven
- Care for self :: care for others
- Minimize conflict :: embrace conflict
- Follow rules :: question rules
- Perfect :: good enough
- Tell :: ask
- Trusting :: skeptical
- Evolutionary :: revolutionary
- Think :: feel
- Urgent :: patient
- Disrupt :: stabilize
- Wield power :: share power
- Guide :: empower
- Exude competence :: exude warmth
- Competitive :: collaborative
- Planned :: opportunistic
- Diplomatic :: candid
- Power in knowing :: power in not knowing
- Analysis :: intuition
- Relationship :: task
- Challenge :: support
- Confidence :: humility
- Leading :: following
- Visionary :: pragmatic
- Accommodating :: demanding
- Daring :: careful
- Calming :: stimulating
- Fast :: thorough

- Directive :: participative
- Individual decisions :: team decisions
- Strategy :: execution
- Efficiency :: effectiveness
- Stability :: change
- Innocent :: political
- Soft-spoken :: forceful
- Fun :: focused
- Focus on results :: focus on process
- Creative :: logical
- Action :: reflection
- Hold lightly :: take seriously
- Appreciate what is :: ask for more
- Develop bonds :: maintain distance
- Diverse :: homogeneous
- Spend :: save
- Form :: function
- Simple :: detailed
- Customize :: standardize
- Formal :: informal
- Broad :: narrow
- Spontaneous :: planned
- Freedom :: security
- Long term :: short term
- Trust in self :: trust in others
- Mission :: margin (common in nonprofits)

Common Family Business Polarities:

- Love :: logic
- Family mindset :: business mindset
- Emotional :: rational

- Belonging :: autonomy
- Invest :: harvest
- Mine :: ours
- Privileges :: responsibilities
- Equal :: equitable (or fair)
- Home :: work
- Hierarchical :: egalitarian
- Centralize :: decentralize
- Independent :: interdependent
- Same :: different
- Cooperative :: competitive
- Long-term investment :: short-term results

Common Succession and Estate Planning Polarities:
- Equal :: equitable (fair)
- Same :: different
- Reveal :: conceal
- Security :: risk
- Go along with the group :: go it alone
- Planning :: action
- Learn by experience :: teach from experience
- Merit :: inherit
- Support :: struggle
- Trust :: control
- Share :: keep
- Tradition :: innovation
- Vulnerability :: protection
- Privileges :: responsibilities
- Cooperate :: compete
- Sooner :: later
- Urgent :: patient

- Proactive :: reactive
- Unconditional acceptance :: conditional acceptance
- Enjoy now :: delay gratification

Common Governance Polarities:

- We :: me
- Flexibility :: structure
- Selective :: inclusive
- Debate :: decide
- Same :: different
- Command :: cocreate
- Unconditional acceptance :: conditional acceptance
- Bottom up :: top down
- Independence :: interdependence
- Enabling :: constraining
- Go it alone :: go along with the group
- Fun :: focused

Common Philanthropy Polarities:

- Live bigger :: give bigger
- Give now :: give later
- My values :: my family's values
- Known impact :: unknown impact
- Planning :: action
- Qualified charities :: unqualified charities
- Direct giving :: indirect giving (Foundations, DAFs...)

"The paradox of education is precisely this—that as one begins to become conscious one begins to examine the society in which he is being educated."

—James Baldwin

CHAPTER 10
APPLYING POLARITY PRINCIPLES TO FAMILY BUSINESS

With the ten polarity principles from chapter 9 in mind, here is a four-step process that enables you to craft a path through the thorniest family business dilemmas. These are designed to support you in finding a both/and approach that harmonizes the tension between opposites. Here are the four steps:

1. Map the polarity.
2. Explore what's possible if you had the benefits of both poles.
3. Identify what feels risky about holding both together. If nothing feels risky, skip to the next step. If you identify risk,
   a. Identify your competing commitments.
   b. Acknowledge your inherent assumptions.
   c. Design relevant, safe-to-fail experiments to test the assumptions. Once you have gathered enough data,

move on to step 4.[94]

4. Brainstorm strategies; then select the one(s) that accrue(s) the benefits of both poles.

Let's practice with one of the dilemmas I mentioned in my introduction: *How do you ensure your sister has the means to survive when the marketplace doesn't value her skills?* This necessitates harmonizing the family mindset, which says *family takes care of family*, with the business mindset, which says *survival of the fittest*.

Imagine this scenario: You are the leader of your family business, and your sister has asked you for a job. She needs the money, and you are torn because her skills aren't well suited to the business world. You are also worried that giving her a job would not only frustrate other employees but would also limit the ability to invest in other areas of the business. At the same time, you don't want to leave your sister high and dry, because you are confident she can't earn as high an income elsewhere.

Let's apply the four-step process to see how it might support finding a path forward.

<u>Step 1: Map the polarity.</u> I have mapped the polarity below. (As a reminder, although I describe the benefits and overuses of various polarities throughout this book, I highly encourage each family to author their *own* polarity maps. The maps in this book are only examples. The benefits and overuses of any polarity will be unique to each family given its circumstances at a point in time.)

---

[94] Step 3, the competing commitments, identifying assumptions, and micro-experiment process borrows heavily from Robert Kegan and Lisa Lahey's wonderful book *Immunity to Change*. This book is a must-read for anyone who finds themselves not doing what they want to do. Robert Kegan and Lisa Laskow Lahey, *Immunity to Change*, (Cambridge: Harvard Business School Publishing Corporation, 2009).

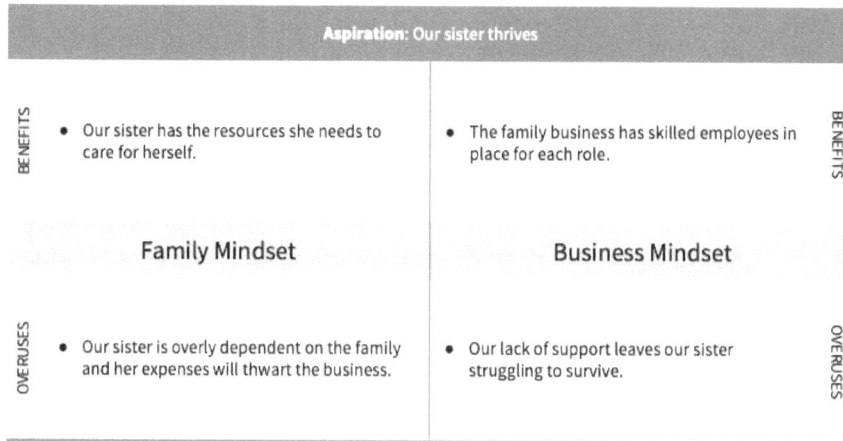

Step 2: Explore what's possible if you had the benefits of both poles. Your sister would have the resources to care for herself, *and* the family business would have skilled employees in place for each role. That should feel quite inspiring!

Step 3: Identify what feels risky about holding both poles together. Your sister might not earn what she needs to live comfortably, or she'll become overly dependent on the family business, which will negatively impact its profitability. Yeesh. Plenty of risk, so let's continue.

Step 3a: Identify your competing commitments. You are committed to a happy, healthy sister *and* to an efficient, profitable business. These are reasonable commitments!

Step 3b: Acknowledge your inherent assumptions. Assumptions in this scenario include:

» If your sister works in the family business, she won't add value commensurate with her compensation.

» If you provide her with the resources to live comfortably, it will thwart the business, and she'll grow dependent on the income.

Step 3c: Design small, relevant, safe-to-fail experiments to test the assumptions.[95] In this scenario, micro-experiments might include:

» Offer your sister a short-term, paid project. This enables both you and her to assess her performance. If she performs well, you can design another project, and another, until she demonstrates her value, and you hire her full time. If she doesn't deliver on the project(s), you have the data you need to have a brave conversation based on facts.

» Offer your sister a small stipend to supplement the income she earns elsewhere in exchange for some part-time work that is not mission-critical to the business. If she thrives in the role, great. If she fails in the role, it won't damage the business.

» Offer to pay for career transition coaching or outplacement services.

Step 4: Brainstorm strategies; then select the one(s) that accrue(s) the benefits of both poles. Harmonizing these poles could look quite different for different families. Here are six different strategies that could harmonize the family mindset and business mindset polarity in this scenario:

1. Agree to a small role for her that won't hurt the business if she underperforms.
2. If she owns shares in the business, issue regular dividends.
3. Ask her to play a role in family governance and pay her for her work.

---

95 Why small experiments? Family businesses are particularly complex systems. A family system is complex in its own right, as is a business system. In a family business, you have two complex systems in a dynamic relationship, creating an even more complex system. Dave Snowden, who developed the Cynefin framework (https://thecynefin.co/team/dave-snowden/), calls complexity the "domain of emergence." Conducting micro-experiments with the family business enables observers to watch how the system responds. This helps families arrive at the next adjacent possible, after which they can design the next micro-experiments. This process continues indefinitely as the family business system is dynamic, not static.

4. Ask her to attend board meetings and pay her for attendance.
5. Supplement her income and accept the decrease in profitability.
6. Create a special needs trust designed to care for her in perpetuity.

Even though we found six ways to craft a both/and strategy to work through this dilemma, these are not the only ways to harmonize these poles. You are limited only by your imagination.

PRO TIP

Once you have found a path forward and are successfully managing the tension of opposites, your work is not complete. Your both/and solutions will need tinkering as your circumstances change over time. Identifying, in advance, the early warning signs that will arise when the strategies you employed to harmonize poles no longer serve the family's interests may help you know when it's time to revisit the polarity. Circumstances may change quickly, generationally, or never.

BOTTOM LINE: OVER TIME, CHANGES TO THE FAMILY AND/OR BUSINESS MAY REQUIRE CHANGES TO THE POLARITY STRATEGY.

Now let's revisit a situation from Polarity Principle #10 in chapter 9: You hear that your niece wants to invite married-ins to work in the family business, and you wholeheartedly disagree. If the question at hand is framed as an either/or—*should we include or exclude married-ins in the employment policy?*—you impose a binary choice: yes or no. It's a false dichotomy. If, however, the issue is framed as a polarity, you bring the right skills and mindset (both/and thinking) to craft a decision that meets your family's current needs. Let's practice.

Step 1: **Map the polarity.** Here again is the sample polarity map from chapter 9:

	Aspiration: Thriving business and family	
BENEFITS	• We limit financial and legal risks in the event of divorce. • We don't have to consider other perspectives that differ from ours.	• Everyone feels like they belong in our family. • We have a larger talent pool to draw from for roles in the business and family governance.
	Exclude — **Include**	
OVERUSES	• Married-ins feel like second-class citizens. • We lose out on valuable skills and insights that married-ins offer.	• A divorce could get more complicated. • We may have to consider other perspectives that differ from ours.
	Aversion: Faltering business or strained family relationships	

Step 2: **Explore what's possible if you had the benefits of both poles:** Everyone would feel like they belong, and we wouldn't have to consider perspectives that differ from our own.

Step 3: **Identify what feels risky about holding both together.** Married-ins might feel like second-class citizens. We may have to consider other perspectives that differ from our own.

>   a. **Spot your competing commitments.** You are committed to fast, efficient decision-making (which is at risk if you have to consider other opinions), and you are committed to making your niece's husband feel like a full part of the family.
>   b. **Acknowledge your inherent assumptions.** If her husband works in the business, he'll have opinions that are different from yours, and it will take time to work through those differences.
>   c. **Design safe-to-fail experiments to test the assumptions.** There are many experiments you could design to test that assumption. Here's one idea: Invite him to weigh in on a

business decision you need to make, but describe the decision using another company as the example. Choose a company in the current news cycle that is facing a similar decision.

Step 4: Brainstorm strategies; then select the one(s) that accrue(s) the benefits of both poles. Here are four different strategies that could harmonize this polarity. How many other ideas can you conceive?

- Define the entry criteria and performance criteria for family employment in a family employment policy. Hold family members, including married-ins, accountable to it.
- Assign him to special projects until he proves himself or the special projects dry up.
- Invite him to participate as an adviser, not an employee.
- Ask him to serve on the family council.

Again, your path to integration of this exclude :: include polarity is only limited by your creativity.

In one final example, let's practice with Wes's situation from chapter 9. As you recall, he wanted to confront his mother about succeeding her as CEO but was reluctant to push her buttons. Here's the polarity map he wrote:

	Aspiration: To become the leader of the family business		
BENEFITS	• I'll maintain a good relationship with my mom. • I'll have more time to learn before taking on responsibility.	• I will know where I stand. • I could lead sooner.	**BENEFITS**
	Cooperate	**Confront**	
OVERUSES	• I'll wait so long that I'll retire before I'm promoted. • The business will lose out on my unique leadership.	• I'll push my mom too hard and damage the relationship. • I'll offend my mom, and she'll retrench in her role, delaying succession.	**OVERUSES**
	Aversion: To stagnate professionally and/or damage family relationships		

Because he understood how polarities work, he started imagining a world in which he enjoyed the benefits of both poles: he maintained a good relationship with his mom, *and* he knew where he stood, *and* he had more time to learn, *and* he shortened the timeline to CEO. This gave him motivation to continue.

From there, he identified what felt risky about holding both poles together. The part he feared the most was damaging the relationship with his mom, which might lead her to *delay* succession. Oof!

Fortunately, this exercise helped Wes identify the understandable, competing commitments that kept him stuck. He realized that, at the core, he was committed to *both* leading the business *and* maintaining a good relationship with his mom. That helped him recognize his unconscious assumption: *if I confront my mom about succeeding her as leader, I will damage our relationship, and she would retrench and delay the succession process.*

Wes's next step was to design a relevant, safe-to-fail experiment to test this assumption. This year, he wanted to lead strategic planning, a responsibility his mother had held for decades. But how should he approach her?

To start, he asked himself whether this was task conflict (people versus problem) or relationship conflict (person versus person). He concluded that this was simply task conflict, so then he decided to use the ALIGN process (from chapter 6): <u>A</u>gree on the goal, <u>L</u>earn the other person's interests, <u>I</u>nvest in their outcome, <u>G</u>enerate ideas, and <u>N</u>othing personal. Here's how his conversation went:

> **Wes:** Mom, you and I have been talking about how to further my growth as a leader, right? (<u>A</u>gree on the goal.)
> **Mom:** Yes Wes. What's on your mind?
> **Wes:** Well, I have some ideas, but before I share them, I'm curious. What are your priorities for this year? (<u>L</u>earn the other person's interests.)
> **Mom:** Well, number one is to execute the agreement to

expand our online distribution, and second, to land the Acme client. Everything else is lower in priority except for spending more time with my grandchildren, but I'm not sure how I'll fit that in with all that's going on this year.

Wes: Yes, important priorities, and I see how busy you are. What can I take off your plate to make room for you to see your grandchildren? (Invest in their outcome.)

Mom: Good question. I don't know off the top of my head. What do you have in mind?

Wes: I've been thinking about it, and I'm interested in facilitating the strategic plan refresh. Leading it could enhance my strategic thinking and facilitation skills, both of which will serve us well in the future. Plus, you'd participate, so I'd get the benefit of learning while you are available for questions. I'd also be interested in setting the board meeting agenda and leading the board meeting on occasion. What other ideas do you have? (Generate ideas.)

Mom: I'm not ready to cede control of the board meeting, but I like your idea of you leading the strategic plan. That would free up a lot of my time. Let's do it. (Nothing personal.)

After a small experiment, Wes learned that his ALIGN approach didn't damage his relationship with his mom. On the contrary, he got exactly what he wanted, and his relationship with his mom remains strong. This micro-experiment strategy allowed Wes to build confidence in his communication skills before engaging on higher-stakes topics. He simply designed experiments until he had collected enough data to build a confident strategy. Over time, his experiments revealed that he *could* harmonize the opposites to get the best of *both* conform *and* confront. Metaphorically, he removed the key he'd kept hidden in his pocket all along to unlock his greater potential.

A Polarity or a Problem?

How do you know when you face a polarity or a problem? When I first learned about polarities, it took me some time to recognize the difference.

First, let's define terms. A problem typically has a solution, a best answer. For example, imagine you are assembling a large airplane engine. Although there may be many ways to assemble this engine, there is one most efficient way. This is a complicated problem that, with thorough analysis, you can identify the solution.

A polarity is a pair of complementary, interdependent values. You face a polarity when one pole exists in ongoing tension with the other pole. Wet doesn't exist without dry, and vice versa. Invest doesn't exist without harvest, and vice versa. Far too often, polarities are framed as either/or problems ("Should we specialize *or* diversify?"), which unnecessarily constrains answers to a yes or no. So, when you hear an either/or question, pause and ask yourself if you face a problem or a polarity.

Another hint that you may be facing a polarity is when you hear a suggestion that surprises you because you'd make the opposite recommendation. For example, suppose your spouse suggests that you fund a 529 Plan[96] for your grandchild using your year-end bonus, but you'd rather get a super yacht in the Caribbean for a week. You may be facing a polarity such as spend :: save. Your preference is to spend; your spouse's preference is to save. Does this need to be an either/or decision? Probably not.

Here are some more examples to discern the difference between a problem and a polarity:

"Should we buy a crane or a tractor?" Problem or polarity? Problem. You can have a crane without a tractor and vice versa. These strategies are not interdependent, so run an analysis to answer this question.

....

96 A 529 plan is a US-based tax-advantaged savings plan designed to help pay for education.

"Should we manufacture in India or Mexico?" Problem or polarity? Problem, because India and Mexico aren't interdependent pairs that define each other, so solve it with analysis. However, consider "Should we manufacture offshore or within country?" Polarity! Polarity, because offshore and within country are interdependent pairs. Each doesn't exist without the other, so map the benefits and overuses and seek ways to integrate the poles so you get the best of both. You may still opt for one pole over the other, but at least you can expect to experience the overuses of whichever pole you choose.

Equal and Fair

In the context of passing assets to the rising generation, a recurring question is "Is fair equal, and is equal fair?" The family mindset often defaults to "equal is fair," but the following metaphor reframes that assumption: Imagine three young siblings, one of whom has a peanut allergy. Treating them equally would be giving them each a peanut butter and jelly sandwich, knowing one child will have a potentially life-threatening allergic reaction. That is equal, but not fair. Similarly, administering an EpiPen to all three children would also be equal, but not fair.

We choose fair over equal *all the time*, and for good reasons. So if your family is struggling with the equal :: fair polarity, map the polarity and change the question from *Should we pass assets equally or fairly* to *How can we get both the benefits of equal distribution and the benefits of fair distribution*? Polarity awareness transforms what may start as emotional relationship conflict into glorious task conflict, where the family cooperates to address the challenge that's over there, metaphorically across the table.

A Return to Family-First or Business-First

The family-first or business-first question said another way is "when we have to choose between the needs of the family and the needs of the business, which domain should we choose?" Problem or polarity? Clearly a polarity in a family business because the poles define each other, so the answer is "wrong question."

Good polarity management may emphasize family over business (or vice versa) during certain eras, given certain circumstances. The key question is "Is the mix of decisions, over time, contributing to sustaining the broader aspiration(s) we have for this family business?" If not, it may be time to revisit the strategies in place to manage the polarity.

Making *both* the family *and* the business a priority is achievable once you frame it as a polarity. As Carrie Hall and Joe Astrachan wrote in the EY publication, *In Harmony: Family business cohesion and profitability*, "There is no trade-off or sacrifice to be made between focus on the business and focus on the family. In fact, the optimal mix—and what the largest and longest-lasting family businesses in the world do—is focus on both simultaneously. Doing so enhances family cohesion, which increases profitability and succession preparation—two crucial elements for a family business that plans to continue far into the future."[97]

Managing polarities is not a fifty-fifty compromise either. A sorely underleveraged leadership superpower, polarity thinking is being intentional in the collaboration process to find a *better* answer that brings a greater benefit to the greater number.

Mahatma Ghandi viewed democracy not as the greatest good for the greatest number but tyranny of 49 percent for the comfort of 51 percent. Polarity thinking is a more generative way to bring the greatest good to the greatest number. The family businesses that lead with a polarity mindset can model for the rest of society how to lead in complexity, so we more ably bring the greatest good to the greatest number.

Family businesses have deep experience managing one of the most challenging polarities of modern society. The me :: we polarity

---

[97] Carrie Hall and Joe Astrachan, PhD, "In Harmony: Family business cohesion and profitability," EY, 2014, 16.

is a microcosm of the individualist :: collectivist polarity which has defined many national cultures.[98] The systemic interconnectedness of a family business requires that each individual in the family navigate the (often agonizing) tension of *both* doing right for themselves *and* doing right for the family. Perhaps family businesses can show the world how to manage the cultural tension between individualism and collectivism better than many nations do today. So many seem to operate in the overuse of either pole.

---

[98] Kendra Cherry, MSEd, "What Is a Collectivist Culture?" *Verywell Mind*, updated on November 8, 2022, accessed on March 3, 2024, https://www.verywellmind.com/what-are-collectivistic-cultures-2794962.

"Power without love is reckless and abusive, and love without power is sentimental and anemic. Power at its best is love implementing the demands of justice, and justice at its best is power correcting everything that stands against love."

—Dr. Martin Luther King, Jr.

CHAPTER 11
CONCLUSION,
A STEP BACK AND A LOOK AHEAD

In his book *Power and Love*,[99] Adam Kahane writes, "When we pretend that . . . our challenges are simple rather than complex, we get stuck. If we want to get unstuck, we need to acknowledge our interdependence, cooperate, and feel our way forward. We need therefore to employ not only our power but also our love. If this sounds easy, it's not." When leaders undervalue the complexity inherent in a family business, they suffer. This book offers a path through complexity so leaders can experience more of the joys of working in a family business.

Love and power exist in various forms in every family business. While families might ideally express more love than power, and businesses may do the opposite, the reality is that both forces exist in each system. At its core, this book has been about harmonizing love and power in both the family and the business for the sake of more harmonious family relationships and a thriving family business.

---

99 Adam Morris Kahane, *Power and Love: A Theory and Practice of Social Change* (Oakland: Berrett-Koehler Publishers, Inc., 2010), 5.

Paul Tillich was the theologian who inspired Dr. King's articulation of power and love in this chapter's opening quote. Tillich defined love as "the drive towards the unity of the separated" and power as "the drive of everything living to realize itself, with increasing intensity and extensity." This polarity of power and love is a living reality in every human heart. We all want to be fully ourselves, and we all want to be connected—we simultaneously crave both autonomy and belonging. The dilemma of the human condition is our need for both opposites. We are an embodiment of this polarity.

Although Dr. King's context was likely social justice when he wrote about love and power, he succinctly describes the overuse of either one. "Power without love is reckless and abusive," he said. Before you simply accept that as truth, sit with this statement. Can you conceive of a situation where that is not true? It certainly lines up with Lord Acton's famous quote, "Power tends to corrupt, and absolute power corrupts absolutely." This lies close to the heart of our intuitive sense that hard power should be used sparingly in a family business, and only when it comes from a place of love. The most effective leaders love *others* as much as they love *themselves*.

"Love without power is sentimental and anemic," Dr. King continues. Before you simply accept that as truth, sit with this statement. Is it true? In a family business, love without accountability and boundaries gets easily abused. Leaders who overuse love for fear of exercising power might benefit from loving *themselves* as much as they love *others*. It is in this dance of partners that the polarity holds the promise of greater well-being in its fullest sense.

A shared tether to the family's golden goose (the family business) amplifies the tension between autonomy and belonging by layering in a new polarity: the family :: business polarity. Family members without a family business are free to pursue autonomy without a threat to belonging in the family. Family members *with* a family business can suffer a unique tension either from the craving for autonomy due to the complexities necessitated by shared ownership of a family business, or the craving for belonging in the face of the unpopular adjudications required of leaders in a family business.

A business system is complex. A family system is complex. A family business is exponentially more complex due to the interactions of these two complex systems. Each needs the other system to thrive. Yet there are inherent tensions that threaten to imperil each system. Given the complexity involved, family business leaders can throw most traditional business "best practices" out the window.

Best practices won't get you to where you want to go. You need a different tool kit—one that relies on polarity thinking, emergence, and capacity development. Every family develops along its own path, and while it looks like these families are veering from one wild experiment to another, they are, in fact, learning as they go. Every family is muddling through. The ones that succeed simply muddle a bit better than the others.

In Kahane's work as a facilitator for business, government, and civil society leaders to address their toughest, most complex challenges, he concluded that "we cannot address our tough challenges only through driving towards self-realization or only through driving towards unity. We need to do both."[100] Our journey has been to make that insight come alive in your life, the life of your family, and the long arc of your family business.

With heartfelt sincerity, I hope that the stories I shared in this book have provided you with insight and courage. *Hug of War* both highlights the challenges inherent in a family business and offers a clear path through these challenges. I wish you well on your family business journey—to lead with a fuller heart and clearer mind.

---

100   Adam Morris Kahane, *Power and Love: A Theory and Practice of Social Change* (Oakland: Berrett-Koehler Publishers, Inc., 2010), 4.

APPENDIX 1
GOVERNANCE

The purpose of family business governance is to clarify, in advance, the roles, responsibilities, and rights of all stakeholders by balancing the power between the family, ownership, and business domains. Because fairness is such a dominant driver in the family mindset, and fairness about the process supersedes fairness about the outcome, family business governance outlines the *process* for making decisions.

Good governance mitigates conflict, as Otis Baskin from the Family Business Consulting Group describes, "The experience of fairness is driven more by the decision-making process than by the decision itself. People can feel as cheated or second-rate when the shares of a business are distributed equally as well as when they are not." Baskin continues, "When leaders in a family business seek to avoid the complexity of engaging all stakeholders in decisions they often bring on the very conflicts they were trying to avoid. The reality is, when family businesses succeed beyond the founding generation into subsequent generations of ownership and leadership, the dynamics of decision-making need to change."[101]

Good governance ensures the right conversations happen with the right people at the right time. For example, governance documents might stipulate that

- Company employees draft the annual operating plan for approval by the board of directors. Nonoperating family owners aren't involved.
- The family (or family council[102]) defines the family employment policy for discussion with the board of directors, and the policy is reviewed every five years. Company employees are not involved.

Although not everyone in a family has an interest in governance, with the privilege of ownership comes the corresponding responsibility. The learning curve for family governance can be steep, and experienced leaders often take for granted the volume of knowledge accumulated over time. To address this, many families include education and training for the rising generation in their governance design so they gain confidence and feel prepared for the responsibilities of ownership. Good governance will outline what's required to participate in the family business, which helps family members decide whether they even want to participate.

Conversely, with the responsibility of governance comes the corresponding privilege. In addition to decision authority that comes with various leadership positions, governance roles are sometimes paid positions and rotate between family members.

Governance design should change over time to meet the changing needs of the family and/or the business. For the entrepreneurial

---

101 Otis Baskin, "Governance Beats Avoidance for Long-Term Family Business Harmony," *The Family Business Consulting Group*, April 8, 2014, accessed March 3, 2024, https://www.thefbcg.com/governance-beats-avoidance-long-term-family-business-harmony.

102 A glossary of family governance terms appears at the end of this chapter.

generation, governance is usually "whatever Mom or Dad says." In the next generation, siblings share decisions, and by G3, when cousins and multiple generations are involved, complexity grows, and decisions can become knotty, making governance more important than in earlier generations.

One caveat about governance: governance is "necessary but not sufficient" in that it provides meaningful support for families with a healthy culture, but good structure cannot salvage a family suffering from high dysfunction. As highly esteemed family business consultant Matthew Wesley says (riffing off Peter Drucker's quote), "Culture eats structure for breakfast."[103] Investing in a healthy culture means both development of individuals and the group.

COMMON GOVERNANCE TERMINOLOGY

For readers who are unfamiliar with some of the family business governance terminology, here's a brief definition of terms:

IN THE DOMAIN OF *FAMILY* GOVERNANCE

Governance in the family domain defines the shared purpose of the family business: why be in business together? This is an important foundation because, without buy-in to this shared purpose, subsequent decisions about the family and/or business lack a "true north" to guide decision-making. It's the family's responsibility to define and uphold its shared purpose, values, mission, and vision for the business so the business operators are clear on the family's expectations.

Widening the lens beyond family business, family governance is also relevant for family enterprises—families who have sold their business and are stewarding shared assets together for current and

---

103 Matthew Wesley, "Culture Does Indeed Eat Structure for Breakfast," *Family Wealth*, December 1, 2004, accessed March 3, 2024. https://www.thewesleygroup.com/blog/?p=609.

future generations. The scope of responsibility often broadens to include family investments, philanthropy, tax and estate planning, trusts, financial planning, etc.

Family Meeting (or Family Assembly)

Often an annual meeting, the family assembly gathers all members and generations of the family together, regardless of who owns shares. Sometimes, the meetings are split into two age groups. The "adult" meetings focus on learning about the family business, general business skill-building, broader family member updates, and changes in ownership. The "children" meetings focus on developing relationships between siblings and cousins, along with some higher-level learning about the business and any stewardship responsibilities that they may grow into in the future.

The family assembly gives all family members a platform to voice their opinions, grooms the rising generation for future leadership opportunities and/or a board position, and fosters intergenerational connections. When the family has grown too large to make efficient and productive decisions, the family assembly forms a family council, which functions as the family assembly's executive committee.

Family Council

The family council, a representative subset of the family assembly, is the setting for determining the rights, responsibilities, and privileges of ownership. It provides a forum for difficult family discussions, regulates family activity within the business and plans, and prepares for future leadership and ownership succession. Responsibilities may include:
- Crafting and maintaining the family constitution and family charter
- Planning family meetings

- Strengthening loyalty and trust within the family
- Celebrating family traditions and achievements
- Strengthening communication between the family and the business
- Crafting and maintaining policies related to family employment, business education, conflict resolution, dividends, philanthropy, family bank, family communication protocols, and/or qualifications for the board of directors and family council participation.

The family council usually meets a few times per year. It has representation from each branch of a family, as well as from all living generations, so it accurately reflects the composition of the full family. Council meetings are typically held in a professional manner, with clear agendas, meeting minutes, and recording history. Because trust can be so tenuous in a family business, open communication and appropriate transparency is essential.

The roles within the family council, such as family council leader and various committee chairs, provide family members with an opportunity to be family leaders without necessarily being employed by the family business. Sometimes, these leadership positions are paid positions (they can become time-consuming!), and they often rotate within the family.

Family Constitution

The family constitution is the written documentation of the family's shared purpose, mission, vision, and values, and it outlines how the family will make important decisions. It is typically amended by the family council, subject to approval from the family assembly. Because of the overlapping impact on the business, the constitution is sometimes drafted in consultation with the company board. The family constitution includes the family council charter (see below), which documents the family council's governance agreements. Although not a perfect analog, the family constitution can be to the family what bylaws can be to the company's board.

Family Charter

The family charter captures the family's agreements in the form of policies. To ensure clarity on the process, many family councils create a family charter that documents the governance agreements—the who, what, when, where, and how decisions will be made within the family council. This includes who votes, what threshold must be met for a decision to pass, where and how often policies can be changed, etc. The charter may also include guidelines on codes of conduct, family employment policy, operations, funding, budgets, family accountability, and role descriptions. Examples include the family employment policy, which outlines the conditions under which family members work in the business, and the vacation home policy, which outlines how family members agree to share vacation home(s).

Family Office

The family office is an administrative and investment center, overseen by the family council, that typically houses the family philanthropy, family bank (loans and investments in family member ventures), trusts, taxes, insurance, estate planning administration, and other administrative functions that serve the needs of the family (such as maintaining family vacation homes and other shared assets). To prepare for sudden or planned generational transfers of ownership, the family office usually ensures that family members have written estate plans, and the business has emergency and long-term succession plans in place.

The family office often employs nonfamily members and maintains relationships with the family's external advisers, such as attorneys, accountants, coaches, financial advisers, psychologists, concierge medicine centers, drug/alcohol rehab centers, and assisted living facilities. Because single-family offices can be expensive to maintain, many families choose to leverage the services of multifamily offices that specialize in efficiently serving the needs of many families concurrently.

IN THE DOMAIN OF *BUSINESS* GOVERNANCE

As family businesses mature, so does their corporate governance. In the founder stage, decisions tend to be unilateral and informal. As ownership becomes more distributed, oversight typically evolves into a family-only board, an advisory board, and eventually a fiduciary board with formal legal responsibilities.

The purpose of the family business board is to represent the interests of the shareholders (usually the family owners) who set direction on risk/leverage tolerance, significant merger/acquisition/divestiture activity, board composition, expected investment returns, share dilution, and core values.

The board holds management accountable for developing and delivering on a strategy that supports the vision, mission, and values set forth by the shareholders. It sets business policy, ensures proper succession planning, monitors family involvement, evaluates liquidity alternatives, sets CEO compensation, and assesses CEO (and sometimes executive team) performance. The ideal board stays strategic, not operational.

Because there can be some overlap between the family and ownership governance responsibilities, good coordination and communication support collaborative decision-making across governance domains.

Advisory & Fiduciary Boards

Advisory boards and fiduciary boards differ in significant ways. Advisory boards give advice that the management team is not obligated to take. Often supplementing the leadership team's skills and knowledge, advisory board members do not have any fiduciary responsibility and are not authorized to request information from management. They see only what management chooses to share, and they have no formal mechanism for holding management accountable.

Fiduciary boards have legal responsibilities, and management is obligated to adhere to the decisions formally adopted by the fiduciary board. Responsible for representing all shareholders, board members accept a duty of loyalty, care, confidentiality, good faith, and prudence. They must disclose conflicts of interest. They have the authority to fire the CEO, and when needed, fiduciary boards develop subcommittees such as finance and audit, compensation, and nominating and governance for focused attention.

Advisory boards are often an interim step between a family-only board and a full fiduciary board with independent-majority members. The advisory board helps the family see the value of shifting control outside of the family and—in the process—builds trust that the fiduciary board's duty is to serve shareholding family members. Family leaders who cede power to independent third parties can enable accountability, improve trust, and augment credibility within a family.

Board Member Selection

Selecting independent third parties is a governance challenge in itself. Trust is built when board members are truly independent—and trust is at risk when board members are perceived as cronies of one or more factions within a family. The less entangled the board member, the more independent she/he is perceived to be.

Independent board members are asked to bring unbiased, objective perspectives. The right mix of independent board members brings fresh strategy, broadened industry networks, cross-industry best practices, and challenging questions.

Selecting which family members serve on the board can raise tensions, and educating family members about their fiduciary responsibilities takes time. Some family members serving on fiduciary boards mistakenly serve their own interests instead of representing the interests of all shareholders, which puts them at risk of violating their fiduciary duties. Serving on a fiduciary board is a substantial responsibility.

IN THE DOMAIN OF *OWNERSHIP* GOVERNANCE

When ownership is not entirely contained within the family, separate ownership governance can exist. Unless managed within the family domain, the ownership domain governs what business to be in, the expectations for return on capital, shareholder risk tolerance, stipulations in buy-sell agreements, shareholder meetings, and expectations for shareholder liquidity needs. It may also establish the ownership criteria for family members, maintain a shareholder agreement in support of succession objectives, and provide a forum for discussing wills and estate planning.

APPENDIX 2
FAMILY BUSINESS POLARITY ASSESSMENT

If you are curious to learn how well you are leveraging the family mindset :: business mindset polarity in your family business, visit https://www.legacyonward.com/assessment to take an assessment.

ACKNOWLEDGMENTS

Without the support of Dave Goetz and Melissa Parks at Journey Sixty6, this book would not exist. My gratitude to them both is endless. They provided support in countless ways, especially in building my confidence that this book is worth writing, encouraging me not to give up, developmentally editing, and sharing publishing knowledge, marketing support, and plain old horse sense. Thank you both!

To me, Matthew Wesley is a wise owl, a provocative questioner, a generous coach, and a brilliant friend. Without him, this book would not have been completed. With decades of experience working with some of the most prominent families in the world, Matt personifies the ideal combination of challenge and support, and I am humbled by his willingness to be a companion on this journey.

To my friends and pre-readers, thank you for your honesty in highlighting what worked and what needed refinement. I'm especially grateful to Garrick Isert, who gently nudged me forward for years, Nicole Lev-Ross for her capacity for detail and personal experience with family business dynamics, Melissa Mitchell-Blitch for her enthusiasm, wisdom, and generosity, and Kristen Heaney, whose keen insights on the family enterprise side of polarities was invaluable.

Great appreciation goes to everyone I interviewed and to those who introduced me to a family business leader for an interview about their experiences as a family business leader. Special gratitude goes to Bill Snow and Clay Garner, who generously shared their networks with me. Without their support, I wouldn't have nearly enough data to identify themes and patterns in family business leadership.

Credit for most of my learning about polarities goes to the following wonderful teachers: Cliff Kayser of Polarity Partnerships, Kelly Lewis and Brian Emerson of Andiron, and Beena Sharma from Vertical Development Academy.

Last, without my wonderful husband, Ken, this book would not be readable. He keeps me calm when I get frenzied, fed when I get hungry, and lighthearted when I get serious. Knowing I have his unconditional love and support gives me a solid foundation to fly. Marrying him was one of the best decisions I've ever made.

Bibliography

Introduction

² "Emerson, Brian and Kelly Lewis. *Navigating Polarities: Using Both/And Thinking to Lead Transformation*. Washington: Paradoxical Press, 2019.

Chapter 1

⁷ Wikipedia. "Amygdala hijack." Accessed March 2, 2024. https://en.wikipedia.org/wiki/Amygdala_hijack.

⁹ SimplyPsychology. "Fight, Flight, Freeze, Or Fawn: How We Respond To Threats." Accessed March 2, 2024. https://www.simplypsychology.org/fight-flight-freeze-fawn.html.

¹⁰ Antonio Damasio. "The quest to understand consciousness." *TED*. March 2011. Accessed March 2, 2024. https://www.ted.com/talks/antonio_damasio_the_quest_to_understand_consciousness.

¹¹ Wikipedia. "Motivated Reasoning." Accessed March 2, 2024. https://en.wikipedia.org/wiki/Motivated_reasoning.

¹² Jaffe, Denis T. "RESILIENCE OF 100-YEAR FAMILY ENTERPRISES: How Opportunistic Innovation, Business Discipline, and a Culture of Stewardship Guide the Journey Across Generations." *Wise Counsel Research*. Working Paper #5: 100 Year Family Research Project. Sponsored by Merrill Lynch's Center for Family Wealth Dynamics and Governance® Merrill Lynch's Family Office Services and U.S. Trust, Bank of America Private Wealth Management (April 2018): 5.

Chapter 2

[13] Greater Good Magazine. "The Power Paradox." Accessed March 2, 2024, https://greatergood.berkeley.edu/article/item/power_paradox.

[14] Conscious Leadership Group. "Locating Yourself - A Key to Conscious Leadership."

Accessed March 2, 2024, https://conscious.is/video/locating-yourself-a-key-to-conscious-leadership.

[16] Brown, Brené. *Atlas of the Heart*. New York: Random House, 2021.

[19] Kahneman, Daniel. *Thinking, Fast and Slow*. New York: Farrar, Straus and Giroux, 2013.

[20] Wikipedia. "Antonio Damasio." Accessed March 2, 2024. https://en.wikipedia.org/wiki/Antonio_Damasio.

[21] Divine, Mar. "The Breathing Technique a Navy SEAL Uses to Stay Calm and Focused." *TIME*. May 4, 2016. https://time.com/4316151/breathing-technique-navy-seal-calm-focused.

[22] Wilding, Melody. "Beat Stress Like a Navy SEAL With This Ridiculously Easy Exercise." *Inc*. July 19, 2017. https://www.inc.com/melody-wilding/beat-stress-like-a-navy-seal-with-this-ridiculousl.html.

[23] Musho Hamilton, Diane. "Calming Your Brain During Conflict." *Harvard Business Review*. December 22, 2015. https://hbr.org/2015/12/calming-your-brain-during-conflict.

[24] goodreads. "Byron Katie > Quotes > Quotable Quote." Accessed March 2, 2024. https://www.goodreads.com/quotes/132449-when-you-argue-with-reality-you-lose-but-only-100.

[25] Goleman, Daniel. *Emotional Intelligence: Why It Can Mater More Than IQ*. New York: Random House, 2005.

[26] Bradberry, Travis and Jean Greaves. *Emotional Intelligence 2.0*. San Diego: TalentSmart, 2009.

[27] Argianas, Alex. "Adopting Emotional Intelligence In The

Workplace Is More Than A 'Nice To Have.'" *Forbes*. May 4, 2022. https://www.forbes.com/sitesforbesbusinesscouncil/2022/05/04/adopting-emotional-intelligence-in-the-workplace-is-more-than-a-nice-to-have.

[28] Brooks, David. *How to Know a Person: The Art of Seeing Others Deeply and Being Deeply Seen.* New York: Random House, 2023.

Chapter 3

[30] Bradberry, Travis and Jean Greaves. *Emotional Intelligence 2.0.* San Diego: TalentSmart, 2009.

[31] David, Susan. *Emotional Agility: Get Unstuck, Embrace Change, and Thrive in Work and Life.* New York: Avery. 2016.

[32] Brackett, Ph.D., Marc. "How We Feel App." Accessed March 2, 2024. https://marcbrackett.com/mood-meter-app.

[33] Gottschall, Jonathan. The *Storytelling Animal: How Stories Make Us Human.* New York: HarperCollins Publishers, 2013.

[34] Sharmer, Otto. *Theory U: Leading from the Future as It Emerges.* Oakland: Berrett-Koehler Publishers. 2016.

[35] Knight, Rebecca. "How to Increase Your Influence at Work." *Harvard Business Review.* February 16, 2018. https://hbr.org/2018/02/how-to-increase-your-influence-at-work. And Castrillion, Caroline. "How To Build Influence Without Authority At Work. *Forbes.* September [24,] 2023. https://www.forbes.com/sites/carolinecastrillon/2023/09/24/how-to-build-influence-without-authority-at-work.

[36] Nacht, Joshua. *Family Champions and Champion Families: Developing Family Leaders to Sustain the Family Enterprise (A Family Business Publication).* Chicago: The Family Business Consulting Group. 2018.

[37] Stuart, Graeme. "4 types of power: What are power over; power with; power to and power within?" Accessed March 2, 2024. https://sustainingcommunity.wordpress.com/2019/02/01/4-types-of-power.

[40] Matthew Wesley, Family Wealth, accessed March 4, 2024,

https://www.thewesleygroup.com/blog and Nye, Joseph, Jr. *Bound to Lead: The Changing Nature Of American Power*. New York: Basic Books, 1991.

Chapter 5

44 Hughes Jr., James E., Susan E. Massenzio and Keith Whitaker. *The Voice of the Rising Generation: Family Wealth and Wisdom*. Hoboken: John Wiley & Sons, Inc., 2014.

45 Wikipedia. *The Simpsons*. Accessed March 2, 2024. https://en.wikipedia.org/wiki/The_Simpsons.

46 Wikipedia. *Maslow's hierarchy of needs*. Accessed March 2, 2024. https://en.wikipedia.org/wiki/Maslow%27s_hierarchy_of_needs.

Chapter 6

47 Di Loreto, Nick and Alison Isaacson. "Avoiding Conflict Will Only Hurt Your Family Business." *Harvard Business Review*. October 5, 2022. https://hbr.org/2022/10/avoiding-conflict-will-only-hurt-your-family-business.

48 Lencioni, Pat. The *Five Dysfunctions of a Team*. Hoboken: Wiley, 2002.

49 Eisenhardt, Kathleen M., Jean L. Kahwajy, and L.J. Bourgeois III. "How Management Teams Can Have a Good Fight." *Harvard Business Review*. July-August 1997.

50 Mitchell-Blitch, Melissa. *In the Company of Family: How to Thrive When Business is Personal*. Charleston: Eredita Consulting LLC, 2020.

51 Scott, Kim. *Radical Candor: Be a Kick-Ass Boss without Losing Your Humanity*. New York: St. Martin's Publishing Group, 2019.

52 Mitchell-Blitch, Melissa. *In the Company of Family: How to Thrive When Business is Personal*. Charleston: Eredita Consulting LLC, 2020.

53 Grant, Adam. *Think Again*. New York: Viking, 2021.

54 Kilmann, Dr. Ralph H. "Thomas-Kilmann Instrument (TKI)."

Kilmann Diagnostics. Accessed March 2, 2024, https://kilmanndiagnostics.com/assessments/thomas-kilmann-instrument-one-assessment-person.

55 Azizi, Mohammad, Masood Salmani Bidgoli, and Ameneh Seddighian Bidgoli. "Trust in family businesses: A more comprehensive empirical review." Taylor & Francis Online. Accessed March 2, 2024, https://www.tandfonline.com/doi/full/10.1080/23311975.2017.1359445.

56 Mcleod, Saul. "Piaget's Theory And Stages Of Cognitive Development." *Simply Psychology*. Updated on January 24, 2024. https://www.simplypsychology.org/piaget.html.

57 Mallel (Morad), Natalie. "Part 1: How To Be An Adult—Kegan's Theory of Adult Development." *Medium*. September 28, 2017. https://medium.com/@NataliMorad/how-to-be-an-adult-kegans-theory-of-adult-development-d63f4311b553.

58 Rachel Myrow, "When a Visit Home Triggers 'Holiday Regression,'" *KQED*, December 23, 2019, https://www.kqed.org/forum/2010101875033/when-a-visit-home-triggers-holiday-regression.

60 Fisher, Roger and William Ury. *Getting to Yes*. Boston: Houghton Mifflin, 1981. Voss, Chris. *Never Split the Difference: Negotiating As If Your Life Depended On It*. New York: Harper Business. 2016.

61 Zola, Andrew. "fist to five (fist of five)." *Tech Target*. Accessed March 2, 2024. https://www.techtarget.com/whatis/definition/fist-to-five-fist-of-five.

62 Solomon, Lou. "Becoming Powerful Makes You Less Empathetic." *Harvard Business Review*. April 21, 2015. https://hbr.org/2015/04/becoming-powerful-makes-you-less-empathetic.

63 Harley, Shari. *How To Say Anything To Anyone: A Guide to Building Business Relationships That Really Work*. Austin: Greenleaf Book Group Press, 2013. Scott, Susan. *Fierce Conversations: Achieving Success at Work and in Life One Conversation at a Time*. London: Penguin Publishing Group, 2004. and Patterson, Kerry, Al Switzler, Joseph Grenny, Ron McMillan, *Crucial Conversations: Tools for Talking When Stakes Are High* New York: McGraw Hill, 2011.

65 Brooks, David. *How to Know a Person: The Art of Seeing Others Deeply and Being Deeply Seen.* New York: Random House, 2023.

66 Mitchell-Blitch, Melissa. *In the Company of Family: How to Thrive When Business is Personal.* Charleston: Eredita Consulting LLC, 2020.

67 goodreads. "Brené Brown > Quotes > Quotable Quote." Accessed March 2, 2024. https://www.goodreads.com/quotes/8404453-daring-to-set-boundaries-is-about-having-the-courage-to-love.

68 Paul, Joe. "Balancing the Emotional Ledger: Axioms and Guidelines for Counseling Families in Business," *Aspen Family Business Group*, https://www.aspenfamilybusiness.com/family-business-publications/bookstore/books/balancing-the-emotional-ledger.

69 Wesley, Matthew. "The Levels of Conflict: A Diagnostic Approach." *Family Wealth.* May 20, 2013. Accessed March 3, 2024. https://www.thewesleygroup.com/blog/?p=404.

Chapter 7

70 Stalk, Jr., George and Henry Foley. "Avoid the Traps That Can Destroy Family Businesses." *Harvard Business Review.* January-February 2012.

71 Keltner, Dacher. *Berkeley Psychology.* Accessed March 3, 2024. https://psychology.berkeley.edu/people/dacher-keltner.

72 Goleman, Daniel. "What Makes a Leader?" *Harvard Business Review.* January 2004.

73 PwC's 2023 US Family Business Survey. *PwC.* May 16, 2023. Accessed March 3, 2024, https://www.pwc.com/us/en/services/trust-solutions/private-company-services/library/family-business-survey.html.

74 Levinson, Harry. "Conflicts That Plague Family Businesses." *Harvard Business Review.* March 1971.

75 Astrachan, Ph.D., Joe, Torsten M. Pieper, Ph.D., Marnix van Rij and Carrie Hall. "Women in Leadership: The Family Business Advantage." *EY.* 2017.

[76] Mitchell-Blitch, Melissa. *In the Company of Family: How to Thrive When Business is Personal.* Charleston: Eredita Consulting LLC, 2020.

Chapter 8

[77] Pattagos, Ph.D., Alex. "Viktor Frankl and the Statue of Responsibility: Balancing Freedom and Responsibility." *Psychology Today*. August 8, 2019. Accessed March 4, 2024. https://www.psychologytoday.com/us/blog/the-meaningful-life/201908/viktor-frankl-and-the-statue-responsibility.

[78] Davis, John A. Accessed March 3, 2024. https://johndavis.com/three-circle-model-family-business-system.

Chapter 9

[80] Kegan, Robert. *In Over Our Heads: The Mental Demands of Modern Life.* Cambridge: Harvard University Press. 1994.

[81] Campbell, Andrew, Sven Kunisch, and Günter Müller-Stewens. "To centralize or not to centralize?" *McKinsey & Company*. June 1, 2011. Accessed March 4, 2024. https://www.mckinsey.com/capabilities/people-and-organizational-performance/our-insights/to-centralize-or-not-to-centralize.

[82] Schuman, Amy, Stacy Stutz and John L. Ward. *Family Business as Paradox.* New York: Palgrave MacMillan, 2010.

[83] Emerson, Brian and Kelly Lewis. *Navigating Polarities: Using Both/And Thinking to Lead Transformation.* Washington: Paradoxical Press, 2019.

[84] Davis, John A. Accessed March 3, 2024. https://johndavis.com/three-circle-model-family-business-system.

[85] Jonathan Haidt. "The moral roots of liberals and conservatives." *TED*. March 2008. Accessed March 3, 2024.

[86] https://www.ted.com/talksjonathan_haidt_the_moral_roots_of_liberals_and_conservatives.

⁸⁷ Johnson, Barry. *Polarity Management: Identifying and Managing Unsolvable Problems.* Amherst: HRD Press. 1992. Johnson, Barry. *And: Making a Difference by Leveraging Polarity, Paradox or Dilemma, Volume One.* Amherst: HRD Press, 2020. Johnson, Barry. *And: Making a Difference by Leveraging Polarity, Paradox or Dilemma. Volume Two.* Amherst: HRD Press, 2021.

⁹⁰ Emerson, Brian and Kelly Lewis. *Navigating Polarities: Using Both/And Thinking to Lead Transformation.* Washington: Paradoxical Press, 2019.

⁹¹ Ibid.

⁹² Ibid.

⁹³ The Myers-Briggs Company. "Myers-Briggs Type Indicator® (MBTI®)." Accessed March 3, 2024. https://www.themyersbriggs.com/en-US/Products-and-Services/Myers-Briggs.

⁹⁴ Robert Kegan and Lisa Laskow Lahey. *Immunity to Change.* Cambridge: Harvard Business School Publishing Corporation, 2009.

⁹⁷ Hall, Carrie and Joe Astrachan, PhD. "In Harmony: Family business cohesion and profitability." *EY.* 2014.

⁹⁸ Cherry, MSEd, Kendra. "What Is a Collectivist Culture?" *Verywell Mind.* Updated on November 8, 2022. Accessed on March 3, 2024. https://www.verywellmind.com/what-are-collectivistic-cultures-2794962.

⁹⁹ Kahane, Adam Morris. *Power and Love: A Theory and Practice of Social Change.* Oakland: Berrett-Koehler Publishers, Inc., 2010.

¹⁰⁰ Ibid.

¹⁰¹ Baskin, Otis. "Governance Beats Avoidance for Long-Term Family Business Harmony." *The Family Business Consulting Group*, April 8, 2014, accessed March 3, 2024, https://www.thefbcg.com/governance-beats-avoidance-long-term-family-business-harmony.

¹⁰³ Wesley, Matthew. "Culture Does Indeed Eat Structure for Breakfast." *Family Wealth.* December 1, 2004. Accessed March 3, 2024. https://www.thewesleygroup.com/blog/?p=609.

www.ingramcontent.com/pod-product-compliance
Lightning Source LLC
LaVergne TN
LVHW041919070526
838199LV00051BA/2664